W9-DBE-058

1/98
GAYLORD F

Map from Goode's World Atlas
© 1996 by Rand McNally, R.L. 96-S-127

Map from Goode's World Atlas
© 1996 by Rand McNally, R.L. 96-S-127

Enchantment of the World

TIBET

By Ann Heinrichs

Consultant for Tibet: Bhuchung K. Tsering, International
Campaign for Tibet, Washington, D.C.

CHILDREN'S PRESS®
A Division of Grolier Publishing
New York • London • Hong Kong • Sydney
Danbury, Connecticut

Left: Mount Everest, the world's tallest mountain, is visible from Rongbuk Monastery, the world's highest, located at 16,500 feet (5,029 meters).

Right: Central Tibet is a flat plateau with many rivers.

Project Editor and Design: Jean Blashfield Black
Photo Research: Jan Izzo

Library of Congress Cataloging-in-Publication Data

Heinrichs, Ann.
     Tibet : enchantment of the world / by Ann Heinrichs.
        p. cm.
     "Age 11-14, grade 6-9."
     Includes index.
     Summary: An overview of Tibet, Roof of the World, whose cruel takeover by the Chinese in 1951 began the darkest period in that country's history.
     ISBN 0-516-20155-7
     1. Tibet (China)--Juvenile literature. [1. Tibet (China)] I.Title.
     DS786.H45 1996
     951'.5--dc20   96-12389
                                                                   CIP
                                                                    AC

Photo Credits ©: Tony Stone Images: Cover, pp. 8, 26 bottom right, 43, 60 left, 66 (Bushnell/Soifer), 18 right (Allan Bramley), 26 top, 29 (Andrew Errington), 26 bottom left, 49 right, 61, 78 (Keren Su); AP/Wide World: pp. 92 top, 101 (both photos), 106, 113; Archive Photos: pp. 95, 107 (Popperfoto); Art Resource: pp. 41 right, 114 top, 135 (Erich Lessing); Asia Access: pp. 34, 73, 123 (Jeffrey Alford), 35, 46 right, 63 (Naomi Duguid); Corbis-Bettmann: pp. 68, 74 left (Reuters), 96 left (UPI), 104 inset (AFP), 89; Jim Cronk: pp. 32 right, 64; Impact Visuals: p. 62 (Sean Sprague); International Campaign for Tibet: 104 top left; Nancy Jo Johnson: pp. 12 right, 14, 18 left, 23, 24, 31, 32 left, 45 left, 49 left, 57 bottom right, 59, 60 right, 90, 128 bottom left, 137; Bonnie Kamin: pp. 19, 58 right, 81, 120 left (Colin Monteath), 36 (John Cleare), 58 left, 134 left (Chris Bradley); Kirkendall/Spring: pp. 98, 119 right, 133; mga/PHOTRI: pp. 4, 45 right, 119 left, 120 right, 132 right (Brent Winebrenner); Patrick Morrow: pp. 6, 13, 16 right, 46 top left, 53, 57 bottom left, 96 right, 117, 128 bottom right, 136, 138; North Wind Picture Archives: pp. 77, 87; Odyssey Productions: pp. 39 top right, 40, 52, 126 (Russell Gordon); H. Armstrong Roberts: pp. 55, 125 right, 128 top (K. Scholz), 92 bottom (Camerique), 65; Root Resources: pp. 21 top left (Anthony Mercieca), 38 right, 41 left, 85, 114 bottom, 125 left (Jane P. Downton); Galen Rowell: pp. 5, 9, 10, 15, 16 left, 17, 21 bottom left, 28, 30, 38 left, 39 left and bottom right, 44, 46 bottom left, 50, 57 top left and top right, 69, 70, 74 right, 79, 80, 83, 103, 108, 110, 111, 121, 130 (both photos), 131, 132 left, 134 right, 141; Tom Stack & Associates: p. 21 center (Brian Parker); Visuals Unlimited: pp. 21 bottom right (Leonard Lee Rue III), 48 (Tim Peterson); The Wildlife Collection: pp. 12 left, 21 top right, 22 left, 25 (Martin Harvey), 22 right (Tom Vezo).
Map of Historical Tibet: George Stewart

Cover picture: The Dalai Lama's Potala Palace

TABLE OF CONTENTS

Chapter 1   *Shambhala* 7

Chapter 2   *Roof of the World* (Topography and Regions, Mountains, Rivers and Lakes, Climate, Animals, Plants, Deforestation *11*

Chapter 3   *The People* (Language, Education and Literacy, Health and Medicine) *27*

Chapter 4   *Daily Life and Customs* (Food and Drink, Dress, Houses, Marriage and Family, Nomads and Their Yaks) *37*

Chapter 5   *Religion, Culture ,and Arts* (Bön, Buddhism, Deities and Symbols, Devotional Practices, Monks and Monasteries, Traditional Arts and Crafts, Literature, Performing Arts, The Calendar, Festivals and Holidays). *51*

Chapter 6   *A Buddhist Kingdom* (The First Yarlung Kings, Songtsen Gampo, The Buddhist Revival, Mongol Overlords) *71*

Chapter 7   *The Rule of the Dalai Lamas* (The Gelukpa Sect, The Dalai Lamas, The Great Fifth, Manchus versus Mongols, The Great Game, The Thirteenth Dalai Lama Modernizes) *79*

Chapter 8   *Tibet under China* (Chinese Invasion, Lhasa Uprising, "Democratic Reforms," A Nation Among Nations, Cultural Revolution, Bitten by a Snake, Still not Happy, Still not Free, The Struggle Continues) *93*

Chapter 9   *The Dalai Lama and the Exile* (The Search, Pleas and Proposals, Government-in-Exile, The Constitution, Around the World) *105*

Chapter 10   *Government and Economy* (Government Under China, The Military, The Economy, Industry, Agriculture, Resources, Transportation, Communications) *115*

Chapter 11   *Monasteries, Temples, and Treasures* (Lhasa, Central Tibet, Tsang, Ngari, Kham, Amdo, The Future) *129*

Mini-Facts at a Glance. *143*

Index *154*

The mountains of Tibet seem to rise out of the mists.
Is this ancient kingdom, now taken over by China, the
hidden kingdom of Shambhala of ancient Buddhist writings?

Chapter 1

SHAMBHALA

Ancient Buddhist writings tell of a hidden land in central Asia, beyond the mountains in the land of the snows. It is an enchanted kingdom, a perfect paradise of matchless beauty. The inhabitants possess knowledge and powers far beyond those in the natural world. And they live in peace, untouched by the evils of civilization. There is no hunger, no crime, no suffering, and no time. No one grows old there, and no one dies. The name of this mystical land is Shambhala. Some call it Shangri-La.

Shambhala is believed to be hidden in the mountains of Tibet. Ancient guidebooks tell exactly how to find this secret land. The instructions are so detailed, they seem surely to be firsthand accounts. Yet, the language of the guides is mysterious, veiled in symbols that few people can understand.

Over the centuries, countless adventurers and spiritual seekers have made the quest for Shambhala. Many lost their lives in the treacherous Himalaya mountains that guard Tibet from the outside world. But Tibet, isolated beyond the mountains, kept its own secrets and nurtured a culture as intriguing as Shambhala's.

Tibetans call their home the "Land of Snows." From the towering snow-covered barrier of the Himalayas, the land slopes northward into the Yarlung Tsangpo River Valley where Tibetan civilization was born. From there, Tibet's warriors and chieftains

Buddhist nuns chant and play drums in their temple in Lhasa.

extended their realm over an area the size of Western Europe. By the seventh century A.D., Tibet's domain reached to the fringes of India, Nepal, Sikkim, Bhutan, and China.

With China and Mongolia to the east and north, and India and Nepal to the south, old Tibet was a crossroads for cultural exchange, despite the mountain passes. Traders brought raw goods, craftsmen brought art styles, and scholars brought new teachings and ideas. This is why the names of people, places, and things in Tibet may have Tibetan, Indian, Mongolian, or Chinese forms.

The greatest gift from India was Buddhism, which Tibetans transformed into a unique Tibetan style. Buddhism, in turn, transformed Tibet. What had been a battleground of warring tribes became a sanctuary for a peace-loving, spiritual people. Before the 1950s, Tibet had over six thousand monasteries, and a monk was the head of state. For Tibet's farmers and nomadic herders, Buddhist devotion sanctified every facet of daily life.

Tibet's evolution has not been easy or smooth, however. Its

Flowers, like hope, continue to bloom in the Land of Snows.

history is marked with warfare and dark intrigue, as rival families and religious sects struggled for power. But no ordeals match the one that grips Tibet today.

Early in the twentieth century, China began moving its borders farther and farther into Tibet. A full-scale Chinese invasion came in 1950. At first, China offered to work with Tibet on friendly terms, but Tibetans got a cruel surprise. In 1959, China struck a crushing blow—a complete takeover, with mass destruction and bloodshed, leaving gaping wounds on the land and in the people's souls. That is where Tibet stands today.

The enchanting Shambhala legend has a dark side. The writings tell of a time when, even in Shambhala, there will be hatred and war. Spiritual forces will battle godless forces for many years until evil is destroyed. Then a spirit of peace and love will reign for a thousand years. Some Tibetans believe that dark period has begun. Their vision of a peaceful future keeps their hope for Tibet alive.

Mount Kailas, in the southwest, is sacred to both Buddhists and Hindus and is one of Tibet's holiest pilgrimage sites. Its snows reflect the setting sun.

Chapter 2

ROOF OF THE WORLD

Tibet is a rugged, mountainous region in central Asia. Geographically, it is one of the most isolated places in the world. High atop a plateau, enclosed by even higher mountains, Tibet occupies the highest part of the Earth. It is sometimes called the Roof of the World.

Historically, Tibet covered about one-third of China's present land area. It consisted of the central province of Ü-Tsang, the northeastern province of Amdo, and the eastern province of Kham. Tibetan people and culture still persist throughout this larger region.

Over time, China gradually absorbed parts of Tibet into its own provinces. Most of Amdo became China's Qinghai and Gansu provinces, while Kham went to Sichuan and Yunnan provinces. In terms of present-day political boundaries, as drawn by Chinese officials, "Tibet" refers to the Tibet Autonomous Region (TAR) of the People's Republic of China. It corresponds roughly to historical Tibet's Ü-Tsang province.

Situated in far southwestern China, the Tibet Autonomous Region covers 471,700 square miles (1,221,700 square kilometers). This is about

Left: The primary location for the endangered giant panda is in China's Sichuan province, adjacent to the TAR. Pandas used to be common in Tibet's forests. Above: Yamdrok Tso is the largest freshwater lake in the TAR.

one-eighth of China's total land area.

Chinese territory lies along about half of the TAR's total border. To the northwest is China's Xinjiang Autonomous Region. This land of nomadic Turkic people is better known as Sinkiang Uighur or Eastern Turkestan. To the northeast is China's Qinghai province. Sichuan province lies to the east, and Yunnan province to the southeast. India borders western Tibet. Along Tibet's mountainous southern border are the countries of India, Nepal, Bhutan, and Myanmar (formerly called Burma).

TOPOGRAPHY AND REGIONS

Millions of years ago, the Indian subcontinent was afloat in the ocean, separate from the rest of Asia. Over time, the two landmasses shifted and collided. As they smashed together, the cataclysmic impact forced the Earth's crust thousands of feet

The Chang Thang is home to many drokpa, or pastoral nomads, who graze their sheep herds on the high rocky plateau.

upward. This collision created Asia's Himalayas, the highest mountain range on the planet. Actually, the collision is still going on, but so slowly that it is hardly noticed. The Himalayas grow a few inches higher every year.

Most of Tibet rests upon the high Tibetan Plateau. Encircled by mountain ranges on three sides, it is the highest plateau in the world. It is actually the bed of a massive lake, the Tethys Sea, which covered central Asia more than fifty million years ago.

The northern part of the Tibetan Plateau is called the Chang Thang (meaning "Northern Plain"). It covers about two-thirds of Tibet's land area. This high, desolate plain is relatively flat, with an average elevation of about 15,000 feet (4,572 meters). Parts of the Chang Thang are barren, rocky desert. In some areas, though, snowy mountains, valleys, lakes, and grassy plains give the Chang Thang a haunting beauty.

Tibet's rivers, most of which rise in the mountains, are the main source of water for the nomadic shepherds on the central plateau.

Along its southern and eastern edges, the Tibetan Plateau drops in elevation. This area is sometimes called the Outer Plateau. Here, especially in the river valleys, is Tibet's best agricultural land. Mountain forests grow in the southeast.

MOUNTAINS

The snow-capped peaks of the Himalayas form a natural boundary for most of southern Tibet. Highest among them is Mt. Everest, whose summit lies along the Nepal-Tibet border. Measuring 29,028 feet (8,848 meters), Everest is the highest mountain in the world. Tibetans call it *Chomolungma,* meaning "Goddess Mother of the World."

Several other record-setting peaks straddle Tibet's border with Nepal. They are Lhotse I, the world's fourth-highest mountain (27,923 feet; 8,511 meters); Makalu I, the fifth (27,824 feet; 8,481 meters); Lhotse II, ranking sixth (27,560 feet; 8,400 meters); and Cho Oyu, the ninth-highest peak (26,750 feet; 8,153 meters).

The Himalayas curve around to form most of Tibet's western edge. There, at Tibet's northwestern border with India, the jagged

Cho Oyu, ninth-highest peak in the world, on the border with Nepal, is visible from the faraway plains around Tingri.

mountains are called the Karakorams, or Mustagh.

The Kunlun Mountains outline the northern edge of the Tibetan Plateau, forming much of the TAR's northern boundary. Historically, Tibetan territory extended even farther north to the Altyn Tagh and Nan Shan ranges.

The Kailas Range of southwestern Tibet runs parallel to the Himalayas. Several of its peaks are higher than 20,000 feet (6,096 meters). The highest is Mt. Kailas, at 22,027 feet (6,714 meters).

Mountain ranges in southeastern Tibet run in a north-south direction, creating a barrier to travel. The major range in this region is the Khawakarpo (the Hengduan, in Chinese).

RIVERS AND LAKES

The Yarlung Tsangpo River flows from west to east across southern Tibet. Its Indian name is Brahmaputra. With its many tributaries, the Yarlung Tsangpo is Tibet's largest river system. Its

Tibet's mountains are the source of two of the world's great rivers, the Brahmaputra (left) and the Indus (right). Both rise in the Kailas mountain range.

waters originate in the Kailas Range and flow through Tibet for some 1,278 miles (2,057 kilometers). It continues its course into India and Bangladesh, eventually emptying into the Bay of Bengal. The Lhasa River (called the Kyichu in Tibetan), on which stands the capital city of Lhasa, is a tributary of the Yarlung Tsangpo.

Headwaters of the Indus, Sutlej, and Ganges rivers also rise in the Kailas Range of western Tibet. They become significant waterways on the Indian subcontinent.

Major rivers in eastern Tibet are the southward-flowing Salween, Mekong, and Yangtze rivers. (Their Chinese names are Nujiang, Lancang Jiang, and Jinsha Jiang, respectively.) These rivers course through the eastern mountain ranges with swift and powerful currents and tremendous drops in elevation.

Rivers on the Chang Thang are small. Their waters, made up

Shown here at twilight, Lake Manasarovar, or Mapham Tso, in the southwest is a holy site to the Buddhists.

of melting glaciers and snowfall, either dwindle away in the desert or feed small lakes.

More than 1,500 lakes are scattered through Tibet. Many are salty, caused by the high concentration of mineral salts in the soil. Kokonor (Mongolian for "sky-blue lake") is the largest lake in historical Tibet and the largest in all of China. Its salty waters fill a basin in the Nan Shan mountains. Nam Tso, northwest of Lhasa, is the largest lake in the TAR and the second-largest saltwater lake in China. Yamdrok Tso, south of Lhasa, is the TAR's largest freshwater lake.

Mapham Tso, a freshwater lake in the southwest, is one of Buddhism's holiest sites. Also known as Lake Manasarovar, it reflects the glistening peaks of Mt. Kailas, to the north.

Hundreds of lakes are scattered across the Chang Thang, remnants of the ancient Tethys Sea. According to Buddhist tradition, these lakes are the tears of Tara, the goddess of compassion. Salty deposits in the numerous dry lake beds have provided Tibetans with salt for centuries.

Tibet does not get monsoon winds, but it still has rainy seasons in the mountains (left). High-altitude desert areas (right) are found in the north.

CLIMATE

Tibet is blessed with abundant sunshine and clear skies, but temperatures can be extreme. Even within one day, it can be 100 degrees F. (38° C) in the afternoon and below freezing at night.

December, January, and February are Tibet's coldest months. In the north and west, wintertime temperatures can plunge to –40 degrees F. (–40° C). May and June are generally the mildest months of the year. In the Lhasa area, the average June temperature is 63 degrees F. (17° C). December's average is 32 degrees F. (0° C).

Central Tibet receives only about 15 to 20 inches (38 to 50 centimeters) of precipitation (rain and snow) a year. The farther north one goes in Tibet, the less rainfall there is. The north and west are the driest areas.

In July and August, fierce rain-filled winds called monsoons

The welcome rains of the Yarlung Tsangpo River Valley allow the cultivated terraced hillsides to produce good crops of barley and mustard.

rip through regions south of the Himalayas. The mountains protect Tibet from the winds, but July and August are still rainy months. About half of Tibet's annual rainfall occurs at that time.

In the Land of Snows, much of the snow remains on the ground all year round. Even in the summer, the permanent snow-line—above which the snow never melts—is between 16,000 and 20,000 feet (4,878 and 6,096 meters). In the south and east, rain-storms and melting snow sometimes cause mudslides and floods.

ANIMALS

The forests of Tibet are home to black bears, red pandas, musk deer, barking deer, and squirrels. Other forest animals are tigers, snow leopards, lynxes, and martens. Monkeys such as rhesus macaques and langurs live in the warmer forest zones. The Tibetan brown bear of the southern forests stands nearly 6 feet (2 meters) tall.

Tibetan antelopes, gazelles, and wild asses (kiangs) graze on the grasslands of the Tibetan Plateau. The antelopes grow horns as long as 28 inches (70 centimeters). Wild asses are very speedy runners and trot across the plateau in huge herds. Wild oxen and wild horses also move in herds. The blue sheep and the ibex, or alpine wild goat, can be seen on high, rocky mountainsides.

The Himalayan marmot, also called the snow pig, is a familiar rodent on the high plateau. Snow pigs sit up on their hind legs like gophers. They make long burrows into the ground, where they hibernate during the bitter winter months. Some other Tibetan rodents are pikas and Himalayan mouse hares.

There are more than five hundred bird species in Tibet. Snow finches, Tibetan rose finches, doves, robins, pipits, and wheateaters are common bird species. Griffon vultures soar above even the tallest Himalayan peaks. Snow grouse inhabit the permanent snow regions all year round, while sunbirds live in the warmer regions. Bar-headed geese, ruddy shelducks, brown-head gulls, and swans breed along the riverbanks and lake shores.

Salmon live in some of Tibet's rivers and lakes. A carp without scales, called the naked carp, inhabits saltwater lakes. Some lakes are so salty that no fish can live in them.

Because of the high altitude and harsh climate, there are few insects in Tibet. However, a tiny brown caterpillar called the aweto has been found at very high elevations. In both Tibetan and Chinese traditional medicine, the aweto is made into a tonic for curing various ailments.

The mythical snow lion is the guardian animal of Tibet. Today, a real cat, the snow leopard, is in danger of becoming just a memory. More than thirty animal species in Tibet are classified as

Tibet has abundant wildlife. Seen here (clockwise from above) are the Asiatic black bear (which is not necessarily black); the Hanuman langur, or leaf-eating monkey; the Tibetan golden pheasant; the ibex of the high mountains; and the Asian wild ass, or kiang, seen here in a valley in western Tibet.

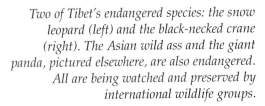

Two of Tibet's endangered species: the snow leopard (left) and the black-necked crane (right). The Asian wild ass and the giant panda, pictured elsewhere, are also endangered. All are being watched and preserved by international wildlife groups.

endangered. Besides the snow leopard, they include the giant panda, Asian wild ass, black-necked crane, wild yak, white-lipped deer, and Tibetan antelope. Snow leopards have been hunted for their fur, and eggs of the black-necked crane have been collected as a delicacy food.

Several U.S. and international conservation groups carry on projects in Tibet to preserve endangered animals. These include Nam Tso Bird Sanctuary, Chang Thang Wildlife Reserve, and Chomolungma Nature Preserve. Other programs protect the black-necked crane and the musk deer.

Chinese officials report that 115 animal species in Tibet are under state protection, representing 36 percent of all protected species in China. They also report that twelve environmental protection zones have been set up in Tibet, covering 115,830 square miles (300,000 square kilometers).

Rhododendron bushes grow in many varieties and in many places in the varied environments of Tibet.

PLANTS

Plant life is sparse on the Chang Thang above 16,000 feet (4,877 meters). Almost no trees or woody plants grow there, but algae, mosses, and lichens thrive at this altitude. Lichens are able to attach themselves to rocks by excreting an acid that breaks down the rock surface.

Grasslands on the plateau provide pasture for both domestic and wild animals. The Outer Plateau, with its milder climate, is the best agricultural region. Many food crops thrive around the Lhasa River Valley and Shigatse.

There are over three hundred species of rhododendron in Tibet. Spectacular red, pink, and yellow rhododendrons grow in the southeast. On high mountainsides, the lack of oxygen causes rhododendrons to be dwarfed and twisted. Other colorful flowering plants are azaleas, pansies, oleanders, and a pink native flower called *tsi-tog*.

In the river valleys of the south and east are forests of oak, elm, ash, maple, and birch trees. Evergreen species include pine,

A peasant woman in the Tingri Valley, like many people in Tibet, may occasionally use wood as fuel for heating and cooking. Commercial logging, however, has had the most serious impact on Tibet's forests.

spruce, Tibetan fir, Chinese hemlock, and magnolia. Junipers and willows can be seen along the riverbanks. The warmer, subtropical regions support banana trees and tea plants.

Over a thousand types of medicinal herbs grow in Tibet. An extract from the Himalayan rhododendron is used to cure bronchitis. The lichen called usnea secretes an antibacterial acid. Other medicinal plants are ginseng, figwort, seven-leafed grass, and a fern that grows on the daimyo oak.

DEFORESTATION

Deforestation is a devastating problem in Tibet. Over 40 percent of the pre-1950 forests in historical Tibet have been cut. In Kham province alone, forests covered 30 percent of the land in 1950. By 1985, they were down to 18 percent. The felled forests

The red, or lesser, panda, some-times called the Himalayan raccoon, has almost disappeared from the mountains as its preferred habitat—bamboo forest—has disappeared.

were dense and very old, some containing 200-year-old trees. Few new trees have been planted to replace them.

Most of these forests grew on steep slopes, where their roots held the soil in place. Without trees, these slopes suffer severe erosion, landslides, and flooding. When tons of mud slide down into the valleys, it covers up farms and roads. Silt washes from Tibet into some of Asia's largest (and muddiest) rivers: the Yangtze, Huangho (Yellow), Indus, and Yarlung Tsangpo (Brahmaputra). Parts of Amdo province lose 40 million tons of topsoil every year.

Loss of the forests also means loss of a home for many animals. International conservation groups call habitat loss the main threat to many of Tibet's endangered species. These include forest dwellers such as giant pandas and red pandas.

Smiling seems to be a common trait of the Tibetan people. The woman above uses her family's yak as transportation for her child. At left, a nomad's daughter hugs her pet baby yak. Below, a man at a window of his home in Lhasa finds pleasure in a cup of tea.

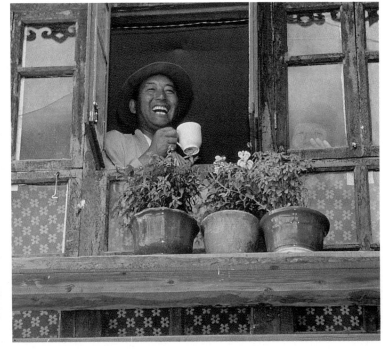

Chapter 3

THE PEOPLE

It has always been difficult to estimate Tibet's population. Because of the rough terrain, many areas simply cannot be easily reached. Tibet's nomads are hard to count, too, because they do not live in a fixed location. More confusion has arisen over the years as China annexed parts of Tibet.

China's 1990 census reported a population of 2,196,010 people in the Tibet Autonomous Region. This makes for an average of fewer than 5 people per square mile (2 per square kilometer). There are an estimated 6 million Tibetans in historical Tibet, including its traditional provinces of Amdo and Kham.

In its census, China does not count all of the ethnic Chinese people who have settled in Tibet. These include technicians, businesspeople, government officials, and military personnel. According to China's 1990 census, there were 81,000 Chinese people in the TAR—less than 4 percent of the population. However, outside agencies figure the number of Chinese in the TAR could be as high as 1.4 million. Most live in the larger cities and towns and in agricultural and industrial centers.

The majority of Tibet's people are concentrated in the south. They live in Lhasa's urban area and in the river valleys of the Yarlung Tsangpo and its branches. Most of the farming, industry, and businesses are in these areas. Almost no one lives in the bleak, frigid northern reaches of the Chang Thang, although about

It's difficult to do a population count of Tibet's nomads because they are continually on the move.

500,000 nomads live along the plateau's outer edges. The Khampas of eastern Tibet and the Goloks in the northeast are nomadic tribespeople.

Lhasa is Tibet's capital and largest city. Its population was about 70,000 in 1950 and 175,000 in 1970. China's 1990 census reported 330,000 people in Lhasa's urban area. It is estimated that Lhasa's population is about 40 percent Tibetan and 60 percent Chinese; that is, three Chinese to every two Tibetan people.

Tibetans are classified in the Tibeto-Burman group of Mongoloid peoples. The 1990 census reported 4,593,330 ethnic Tibetans in the People's Republic of China. Tibetan people live not only in historical Tibet, but also in parts of Nepal, Bhutan, and India. Small pockets of non-Tibetan peoples have traditionally lived in Tibet as well. These include the Qiang, Moinba, Lhoba, Naxi, Hui, Nu, and Drung groups.

From the Chinese point of view, Tibetans are a tiny ethnic minority. They make up less than half of 1 percent of China's total

Pilgrims on a mountain path overlook the cloud-covered city of Shigatse, Tibet's second-largest city.

population (more than 1.1 billion people). In contrast, the ethnic Chinese represent about 92 percent.

The Chinese government encourages Chinese people to migrate and settle in its newly acquired territories. This helps to dilute the native culture and establish Chinese culture. Studies indicate that about 7.5 million Chinese people live within Tibet's traditional boundaries, compared to only 6 million Tibetans. Even in Tibet, Tibetans have become a minority.

LANGUAGE

The Tibetan language belongs to the Tibeto-Burman language group. Other languages in this group are spoken across the Himalayan region. Native Tibetan speakers live in Tibet, as well as Nepal, Bhutan, and India. Several dialects of Tibetan are

Both Tibetan and Mandarin, or Chinese, script are sometimes used in signs.

spoken in the different, separated regions. However, the dialect spoken in the Lhasa area is considered the standard form.

Tibetan first took written form in the seventh century A.D. Thonmi Sambhota, a minister of King Songtsen Gampo, devised a Tibetan alphabet and script based on India's Sanskrit script. The Tibetan alphabet has thirty basic characters, plus four vowels.

There are four styles of written Tibetan: one for Buddhist texts, one for books and other printed material, a cursive script for formal and ornamental use, and an informal script for everyday use. Tibetan characters do not translate directly into the Western alphabet. Thus, Western spellings of Tibetan words often vary.

Tibetan sentence structure follows the order of subject-object-verb. Although Tibetan is not a "tone" language, as Chinese is, the intonation of words is important in communicating meaning.

Bicycles are an important form of transportation in Tibetan cities,
especially for children going to school.

The Mandarin dialect of Chinese is the official language for
business, government, and education throughout China, including
the TAR. Signs, broadcasts, and instructions are in Chinese. This
use of Mandarin is a serious, daily hardship for Tibetan speakers.
Simple activities such as shopping or taking a bus ride can be
nerve-wracking. In some places, loudspeakers are set up all over
town to broadcast Chinese programs from morning till night.

EDUCATION AND LITERACY

Monasteries were once Tibet's primary learning institutions.
Students entered at the age of six or seven and learned to read and
write. They studied not only religion, but also medicine, philosophy, and metaphysics. There was no secular education, except for
apprenticeship programs for artists and craftspeople.

In 1959, the Chinese abolished religious education in Tibet and
set up a secular school system. Chinese became the official
language, and teaching or using the Tibetan language in schools

These nomadic girls (left) will probably not attend school at all, but the fact that they are wanderers will keep them speaking Tibetan. The city boy (right) will grow up with Chinese and even international influences.

was prohibited. In the 1980s, the ban on the use of Tibetan was lifted, but Chinese is still the primary language in the schools. In a few schools, Tibetan language classes can be chosen as a second language after Chinese.

Tibetan parents are disturbed to see their children losing the Tibetan language. Tibetan history and culture are taught only in "patriotic" Chinese versions. Some parents keep their children out of school to keep them from learning Chinese language and values.

Tibet's education system consists of primary schools and secondary schools. Some regions also have middle schools. In general, towns with Chinese residents have schools, while those with only Tibetan residents do not. In 1990, about 22 percent of adults in Tibet could read and write. According to Chinese education officials, 55 percent of the 700,000 children in the TAR attend school.

Tibet University is in Lhasa. There are also a number of training institutes that prepare students to become local administrators
and government officials. All higher education is in Chinese, so a
student must be proficient in Chinese in order to advance.

Some of Tibet's monasteries have reopened, but children may
not study there. Eighteen is now the youngest age at which a
person can enter. The number of monastery students is controlled,
and a person must receive government approval to enter.

HEALTH AND MEDICINE

By nature, Tibetans are physically hardy. Living for centuries
at a very high altitude, their bodies have developed unusual
abilities to survive. Oxygen in the atmosphere decreases the
higher one goes. At an altitude of about 17,000 feet (5,182 meters),
there are only about half as many oxygen molecules as there are at
sea level. Tibetan nomads have more than 20 percent more
hemoglobin (oxygen carriers) in their blood than people who live
in the lowlands.

Activity at high altitudes also burns more calories, so Tibetans
tend not to accumulate fat. Tibetan refugees in other countries
usually find that they have to change their diets because they are
burning fewer calories. Some also acquire heart disease after
leaving Tibet.

Tibetans live shorter lives than do people elsewhere in China.
International agencies estimate that Tibetans' life expectancy may
be as high as 61 years or as low as 40 years. In contrast, the
average Chinese person in 1990 could expect to live 70 years.
Common illnesses include influenza, pneumonia, and tuberculosis.

Children growing up on the high-altitude Chang Thang plateau develop extra oxygen-carrying blood cells.

A Tibetan baby is about three times as likely to die in infancy as a Chinese baby. Many Tibetan women avoid going to Chinese-run hospitals because they fear they will have to undergo sterilizations or abortions.

Many health problems stem from industrialization, which has brought air, water, and soil pollution to Tibet. Water supplies are no longer clean, and water sources near nuclear facilities have become dangerous.

Hospitals and clinics exist in Tibetan towns that have Chinese settlers. There is a shortage of doctors and nurses to staff them, however, so frequently patients in hospitals are cared for by their families. Hospitals practice both Western and Chinese medicine.

Traditional Tibetan medical treatment is available in Lhasa's Tibetan Medical Center, which treats over six hundred patients a day. Over their long history, Tibetans developed a unique medical system. Grounded in ancient texts, it borrows from Indian and Chinese medicine. Tibetan medicine is based on the balance of forces operating in the body. Three "humors"—wind, bile, and phlegm—correspond to the three spiritual poisons: ignorance,

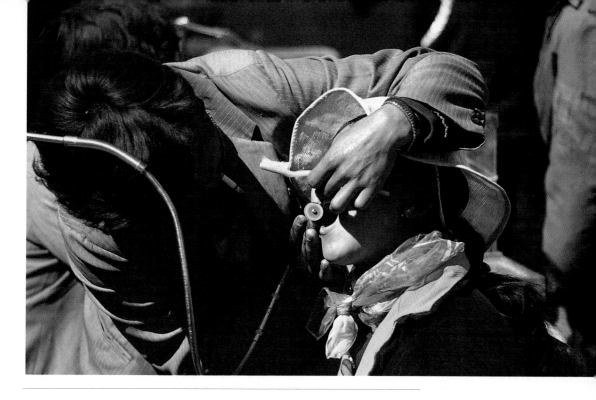

Dentists in Lhasa do their work right out on the street where patients can drop in while working or shopping.

greed, and hatred. Besides the humors, there are three bodily sustainers, seven eliminators, and several hundred spiritual influences. All these can affect a person's health. If they are not in balance, an illness results.

A traditional Tibetan doctor makes a diagnosis by taking "pulses" along any of the 360 channels of energy that run through the body. A good doctor can detect any imbalance and its cause. Disorders are then treated with herbs, acupuncture, or moxibustion (burning mugwort at the free end of an acupuncture needle).

Over one thousand herbs are used in preparing Tibetan medicines and remedies. Parts of various animals are also believed to have healing powers. Some of these are deer antlers, antelope horns, bear gall bladders, tiger and leopard bones, and musk from the musk deer.

Chapter 4

DAILY LIFE
AND CUSTOMS

FOOD AND DRINK

Yak-butter tea is the Tibetans' everyday beverage. They have a few cups in the morning, drink it throughout the day, and serve it to guests. It is prepared by pouring butter and strong tea into a tall wooden churn, adding some salt, and churning the mixture until it is thoroughly blended. Tea should be sipped; it is improper to gulp down the whole cup at once. A guest's cup should always be kept full. *Chang,* or barley beer, is a common beverage for social and festive occasions.

Tsampa is the staple food. It is roasted barley, often mixed with peas and ground into flour. Tsampa may be blended with butter tea to make a dough and rolled into balls. Tsampa boiled in water with meat and vegetables makes a tasty stew.

Nomads prepare chewy strips of dried yak or lamb meat. Because of the limited oxygen at high altitude, meat does not spoil for months. *Momo* are traditional meat dumplings. Yogurt, yak

Opposite: Tibetan children enjoy seeing their traditional hand-woven family carpet airing in the sunshine.

Churning yak-butter tea (left) is a daily task for nomadic women. The process thoroughly mixes butter, thickly brewed tea, and salt. Bread is for sale in the open markets of cities (right).

curds, and hard balls of yak cheese round out most Tibetans' everyday fare.

While these are the usual foods in the countryside, they are not so common in the cities. Restaurants usually serve *thukpa,* a noodle broth with bits of meat and vegetables. Tea and Chinese beer are the usual beverage choices. Many towns have restaurants that serve Sichuan-style Chinese food and stores that sell Chinese foods such as canned meat, dried or fresh fruits, rice, and biscuits.

DRESS

In cities and towns, many Tibetans wear Chinese or Western-style clothes. Most, however, still dress in traditional styles, with distinctive variations in different regions.

Women wear black dresses or black shirts, skirts, and pants.

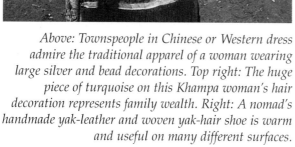

Above: Townspeople in Chinese or Western dress admire the traditional apparel of a woman wearing large silver and bead decorations. Top right: The huge piece of turquoise on this Khampa woman's hair decoration represents family wealth. Right: A nomad's handmade yak-leather and woven yak-hair shoe is warm and useful on many different surfaces.

Over their dresses they wear brightly striped wool aprons. They may wear turquoise hair clasps and hair pins or bright-red braided hairbands with silver ornaments. Some thread their hair with turquoise beads. Others braid their hair in 108 strands in honor of the 108 volumes of Buddhist scripture.

There is an old Tibetan tradition of putting all the family wealth into jewelry. A woman of a wealthy family might have

A Muslim family in a park in Lhasa is dressed in a combination of Western-style and traditional clothes.

worn tens of thousands of dollars worth of precious metals, gems, and pearls at once. That tradition is still apparent, though on a smaller scale. Tibetan women wear earrings, bracelets, necklaces, headbands, belts, amulets, and other religious ornaments. The jewelry is made of silver, turquoise, coral, and amber. Seashells and coral are specially prized because Tibet is so far from the sea.

Men wear a loose shirt and pants. Over this is the *chuba,* a sheepskin or wool cloak slung loosely over the shoulder and tied at the waist. Their high boots are made of yak hide and yak-hair felt. Headgear varies by region and includes stiff felt hats with bright embroidery and ear-flapped wool hoods.

Monks wear burgundy-colored robes. For ceremonial occasions, they wear hats that vary in color and style according to the Buddhist sect to which the monks belong.

Khampa tribesmen braid strands of their hair with red yarn. They carry a dagger at the waist and wear an earring in one ear. According to local tradition, a man who did not wear an earring would be reincarnated as a donkey.

A typical house in the Shigatse region (left) focuses on a stove for warmth.
A typical farmhouse (right) has a wall enclosing several buildings.

HOUSES

A typical Tibetan home has an earthen floor. It stands one or two stories high, with inward-slanting walls made of whitewashed earth, brick, or stone. Some homes are built right up against a mountainside. Windows are covered with waxed paper or cloth, although some have glass windowpanes. The roof is flat and may have a wall around the edge. In some areas, homes are painted in various colors instead of white. Finer homes may have brightly painted roof beams and window frames, decorated wooden doors, and window boxes.

In two-story homes, the first floor is used for cooking, eating, socializing, and storage. A fire of dried yak dung burns inside a brick stove. The family's possessions are stored in carved wooden cupboards and chests. Against one wall is the household altar with statues, religious pictures, and yak-butter candles or lamps. The family sleeps on the second floor.

Most rural homes are lighted only by oil lamps, although electricity is now reaching more areas. Water is drawn from a local stream or well. Indoor plumbing is rare. Generally, people just find a private spot outdoors.

In farming communities, several homes may be clustered together, surrounded by a wall. Other farmhouses are built around a courtyard, with connected barn, stable, and house.

MARRIAGE AND FAMILY

By tradition, a couple's parents arrange their marriage. They consult a monk, an astrologer, or a shaman (a priest-doctor who deals in magic) to determine the best time for the marriage. The couple may hardly know each other. However, if one of them seriously objects to the marriage, it is called off. Among nomads, the parents may arrange the match, but the boy and girl meet each other several times and exchange gifts.

On the big day, the groom and his family dress up and ride over to the bride's home. They stand outside the door calling for the bride to be sent out. Meanwhile, inside, the bride is decked out in her finest jewelry and clothes. She has been collecting ornaments all her life to wear on this day. But she and her family shout for the groom's family to go away. There are protests, scream-ing, and tears. The shrieking bride is tugged this way and that until the groom wins his true love, and off they ride to make a home with his family.

Tibet never had an overpopulation problem because so many Tibetans became monks. Some monks could marry and have families, but those of the majority Gelukpa order take a vow not to marry. After China invaded and destroyed the monasteries, monks were ordered to marry and live like everyone else.

*This Tibetan family has only the two children allowed by Chinese decree.
Like most Tibetan homes, their stone house is decorated with flowers.*

The size of a Tibetan family is controlled by Chinese law.
Families living in towns are allowed to have only two children.
Families in rural areas may have three. Tibetans have reported
paying fines greater than their average yearly income for having
an extra child. In general, Chinese people are allowed to have only
one child per family. However, those who agree to move to Tibet
are permitted to have two.

At a nomad camp on the northern plateau, several families socialize and cook in one large tent, though the families sleep in their own separate tents.

NOMADS AND THEIR YAKS

About half a million Tibetans are nomads, or *drokpa*. They live on the harsh northern plateau in camps of several families each, along with their herds of yaks, sheep, and goats. To keep the herds on good pastureland, they move from place to place. A group may stay in one location for weeks or even months.

Nomads' homes are large tents made of yak-hair felt. The yaks' short, inner hair is soaked and pounded into a tough, sturdy cloth that keeps out the cold and wind. It is stretched over a frame held up with ropes and stakes. A hole in the top lets smoke escape.

Left: A drokpa mother cooks outside the tent while her children play.
Right: Large guard dogs called mastiffs often live with nomad families.

Each tent is the family home and the center of daily life. Near the entrance is a fire pit with a yak-dung fire for cooking and warmth. Against one side of the tent is the family altar, with religious statues and images. Yak-butter lamps are kept burning there night and day. Nearby is a large, intricately carved wooden chest holding family belongings. On shelves or hooks are pots and pans, cooking utensils, tools, ropes, and other supplies. There is a wooden churn for making butter and a loom for weaving rugs, blankets, and cloth.

When it's time to move, the nomads pack up, take down the tents, and load everything onto their yaks. They travel in a caravan to a new pasture, where they set up their homes again.

Many camps keep large, fierce dogs called mastiffs. They guard their masters from bandits and wild animals. Yet the mastiffs are friendly, faithful companions for their owners and gentle playmates for the children.

Sheep, one of the useful animals that nomads herd, need to be milked regularly (top left). The nomads spin their wool (above), and they weave cloth on small portable looms (left).

Nights on the Tibetan Plateau can be bitterly cold, with piercing winds. The nomads often build stone walls around their tents as a windbreak. In some camps, a community fire burns in the center of the settlement. Women and children usually sleep in the tent, bundled in sheepskins and yak-hair blankets. The men often sleep outside near the fire. They may curl up against their sleeping sheep, whose bodies radiate a toasty warmth.

Everyone rises early. Men get the fires going, while women

milk the animals. An offering to the gods of barley grains is burned on the altar. After a breakfast of butter tea and barley cakes or yogurt, the day's work begins.

Men take the herds out to pasture. In the springtime, they may make an expedition to a dry lake bed to collect chunks of salt. Back at the camp, children practice with slingshots, play with the dogs, or help with the chores. Women tan hides, spin wool, sew clothes, weave blankets, strip and dry yak meat, and make butter, yogurt, and cheese.

Trading time is a big event. In the winter, nomads trek to a farming village, where they trade their own products for goods they need. Besides wool, meat, butter, and hides, the nomads bring salt and medicinal herbs gathered on the plateau. In exchange, they get barley, rice, flour, and tea.

"We have a very easy life," one nomad told a researcher. "The grass grows by itself, the animals reproduce by themselves, they give milk and meat without our doing anything. So how can you say our way of life is hard?"

Shaggy domestic yaks are all-purpose beasts. About two million of them graze the plateau. Yaks provide their owners with a wealth of benefits. They climb steep and rocky slopes with heavy loads of trade goods, household belongings, and nomads' tents, which can weigh 200 pounds (91 kilograms).

The female yak, or *dri,* gives sixteen times as much milk in a year as a sheep does. Yak milk is high in fat content and is made into butter, cheese, yogurt, and curds. The butter is used for tanning hides, fueling lamps, making candles and sculptures, and preparing butter tea. People sometimes smear butter on their faces to protect their skin from the biting wind.

The yak, sometimes called the grunting ox, thrives at the high altitude of the Tibetan Plateau.

Yaks' coarse outer hair is made into ropes and slingshots, while the softer inner hair is made into felt for tents and boots. That softer hair is also spun into yarn for weaving clothes and blankets. Yak meat is low in fat. Tibetans eat it cooked, smoked, or dried. Yak stomachs are used as bags for storing yogurt. Yak hides become boots, belts, boats, saddles, and saddlebags. Dried yak dung is the national fuel.

Two other types of yak live in Tibet. Wild yaks are almost twice the size of domestic yaks and have extremely long horns.

The long, tough hair of a yak can be used to make a slingshot (left). Its hide can be used to make a sturdy but light-weight waterproof boat for fishing.

Huge herds of wild yaks used to roam the plateau, but Chinese soldiers killed them for food. Those that remain live in remote areas and are rarely seen today. The *dzo* is a cross between a cow and a yak. The strong, gentle dzo is used as a pack animal or for heavy farm chores.

Sunbeams brighten Samye Monastery near Tsetang.

Chapter 5

RELIGION, CULTURE, AND ARTS

With high mountain ranges isolating it from its neighbors, Tibet developed a unique culture. More than any other factor, religious devotion permeates Tibetan culture, arts, and daily life.

Buddhism is the predominant religion among Tibetans. Some Tibetans practice the ancient Bön religion. There are also small numbers of Muslims and Christians in Tibet. The Hui, who live in Lhasa and other large towns, are Muslims.

BÖN

Before Buddhism arrived in the seventh century, Tibetans followed an ancient folk religion called Bön. Bön is rooted in animism, the worship of spirits in nature and natural places, such as mountains and streams. The Bönpo (Bön believers) have elaborate rituals for appeasing gods, driving out demons, and warding off troublesome ghosts.

Shamanism is another Bön practice. By going into a trance, shamans—who are regarded as priest-doctors—enter the spirit world and battle evil spirits or discover how to treat illnesses.

After Buddhism took hold in Tibet, Bön came to resemble

This Bön monk, devoting his life to a small temple, combines some Buddhist practices with his faith.

Buddhism in many ways. The Bönpo built monasteries throughout Tibet. Buddhism, in turn, built upon Bön and absorbed many of its beliefs and practices. Among the few remaining Bön monasteries in Tibet are Yungdrung Ling and Menri, east of Shigatse. Menri Monastery is the center of Bön culture and teaching. Today there are Bönpo in Nepal and Bhutan, as well as among Tibetan refugees in India.

BUDDHISM

The name *Buddha*—meaning "Enlightened One"—is used in two ways. It can mean a highly spiritual being, or it can refer to the actual, historical figure who founded Buddhism.

Prince Siddhartha Gautama, son of a powerful warrior-chief, was the historical Buddha. He was born in southern Nepal about 563 B.C. and grew up in a luxurious palace surrounded by lush

A huge Buddha has been carved into the cliff alongside the road to Gyantse, west of Lhasa.

gardens. Curious to see the real world beyond the palace walls, he ventured outside for the first time at the age of twenty-nine. The sight of an old man, a sick man, and a corpse changed the prince forever. He left home and began a quest to unlock the mystery of human misery.

After six years, the prince saw the light. The things of life, he realized, are passing illusions. Attachment to these illusions—through desire or hatred—causes both pleasure and pain. Now, as the Buddha, or Enlightened One, he began to preach his Eightfold Path to enlightenment.

Reincarnation is a central doctrine of Buddhism. By the law of karma, or spiritual cause-and-effect, living a good life earns rebirth of the soul at a higher level. The goal of the successive lives is nirvana—a state of perfect enlightenment, the end of suffering, and a release from the cycle of rebirth. Bad living sends a person backward to a lower, more miserable state of being.

Buddhism split into several branches. The Mahayana sect took hold in Tibet and spread to China, Korea, and Japan. It introduced the idea of the *bodhisattva*. This is any person on the path to enlightenment who is dedicated to helping others attain release from suffering. Tibetan scriptures say that, as long as there is even one living creature left on earth, a bodhisattva will be there to help.

(By contrast, the Theravada sect concentrates on studying the life of Prince Gautama, the historical Buddha, and various Buddhist scriptures. Theravada is the dominant branch in Sri Lanka and Southeast Asia.)

According to Tibetan Buddhism, compassion is the highest virtue. The three "poisons"—the roots of all suffering—are greed, hatred, and ignorance. Through wisdom and compassion, a person can eliminate these poisons and reach enlightenment. Another facet of Tibetan Buddhism is tantrism, the "diamond path." It involves the practice of *tantras*—meditations and spiritual exercises that bring deep insight and wisdom.

DEITIES AND SYMBOLS

Tibetans are most devoted to Chenresi, the bodhisattva of compassion. (Avalokiteshvara is his Indian name.) In art he is often depicted with many hands extended, symbolizing his mercy reaching out to all. Jampalyang (called Manjushri in India), the bodhisattva of wisdom, wields the flaming sword of wisdom that cuts through ignorance. Chakna Dorje (Vajrapani), the lord of energy and power, holds a thunderbolt. Sakyamuni, the historical Buddha, sits cross-legged on a lotus throne. Jampa (Maitreya) is

This statue at Sera Monastery represents a bodhisattva of wisdom who helps people on the road toward enlightenment.

the next Buddha who will come to earth in human form. Tibet's patron goddess, Dolma (Tara), represents the female aspect of compassion. Other gods represent such virtues and activities as purity, creativity, healing, and long life.

The Eight Auspicious Symbols are gifts that the Buddha received upon attaining enlightenment. They include the Lotus

Flower, signifying purity and compassion; the Two Golden Fishes, leaping from the swirling waters of life's cycles; and the Eight-Spoked Golden Wheel, representing the Noble Eightfold Path.

A *mandala* is a design with a central deity encircled by other beings and symbols that make up his or her world. Mandalas often appear in Tibetan art. There is also a ritual in which monks create a mandala as a spiritual exercise. Using grains of colored sand, they meticulously construct an intricate design on the floor. Then, by meditating on the completed mandala, they merge with the deity it represents. Last of all, the sand is swept up and poured into a river.

DEVOTIONAL PRACTICES

Circumambulation—praying while walking round and round a holy place—is common to both Buddhism and Bön. The Bönpo walk in a counterclockwise direction, while Buddhists make a clockwise circuit. Many pilgrims travel in prostrations—that is, by stretching out on the ground for their full body's length, rising, stepping to where their head had been, and stretching out again.

Prayer wheels are cylinders with prayers written on pieces of paper coiled inside. They may be small, hand-held devices or huge drums placed along the walls of a shrine. Every rotation of the wheel is considered a recitation of its prayer. Prayer flags, seen fluttering from branches and rooftops, work on the same principle. These are swatches of colored cloth printed with prayers. Every breeze that ripples the flag sends the prayer heavenward. Prayer flags are found on even the most remote mountains.

Reciting the mantra, or chant, *"Om mani padme hum"* focuses

Some devotional practices that occupy much of the life of a devout Tibetan Buddhist include (clockwise from above): circumambulating holy places (the pilgrim above is traveling with his dogs), sometimes done by prostrations—lying full length on the ground; flying flags that represent prayers; and turning giant prayer wheels.

Mani stones (left) are found scattered along pilgrims' paths. In a traditional Buddhist sky burial (right), the crushed body is laid on a special stone slab where vultures wait.

the mind and heart on Chenresi and his attitude of compassion. Mani stones, often seen along pilgrims' paths, are boulders with this mantra carved or painted on them. Rosary beads are used as guides for prayer and chanting. Rosaries are made of 108 stones, representing the 108 volumes of Buddha's teachings.

Barley grains and fragrant juniper twigs are burned as offerings at altars and shrines. Pilgrims may drape a ceremonial scarf *(khata)* around the neck of a statue or present a khata to an honored monk.

Tibetans see the body as a temporary housing for the soul. After the spirit has left, the body's purpose is finished. The remains are recycled, in a way—returned to nature. Since Buddhism arrived in Tibet, sky burial has been the common type of burial. The body is wrapped in a cloth, and family and relatives gather with a monk for final prayers and blessings. Then the body is taken to a high place, where a hired person called a *tomden* breaks up the body. He crushes the bones and mixes them with barley to be left for the ravens and vultures. Nourishing the birds in this way is seen as the person's last act of charity.

The bodies of high-ranking monks are cremated, and their ashes are placed in a shrine. Otherwise, cremation is rare because wood for fire is so scarce. Bodies of the highest lamas are preserved by embalming. Burial in the ground is very rare.

MONKS AND MONASTERIES

Before the Chinese takeover, about one out of every five Tibetans was a Buddhist monk or nun. Every family hoped to send at least one son to the monastery. Boys usually entered at about the age of seven and began years of study. Some monks continued on to higher religious studies, while others were trained as cooks, clerks, artisans, scribes, or even monk-soldiers. The head monk in a monastery is the abbot.

In Tibetan society, monasteries functioned as universities, art museums, charitable foundations, landlords, and lending institutions. Before the 1950s,

A young monk introduces a friend to the book he is learning to read at Kumbum Monastery.

Left: Monks play special horns during a ceremony.
Right: An elderly woman carries out traditional devotions
at a partially destroyed monastery.

there were about 6,200 monasteries in Tibet. The Chinese destroyed almost all of them, leaving fewer than forty standing.

Since the 1980s, some of the monasteries have been rebuilt. Young men are once again allowed to become monks, though in strictly controlled numbers. Many monasteries now have "official monks," who have passed government screening tests, and "unofficial monks," who carry on their devotions without government approval. Monks today complain that there are not enough monks left from the old days to provide proper training and spiritual guidance.

China may have realized that monasteries make a great tourist attraction. Monks in monasteries around Lhasa have reported that, when a tourist bus arrives, Chinese officials direct them to

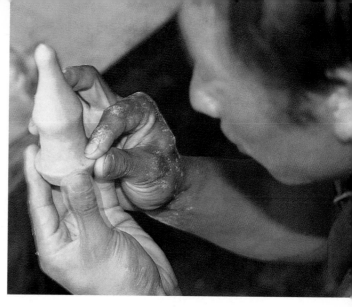

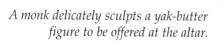
A monk delicately sculpts a yak-butter figure to be offered at the altar.

put on their robes and hats and start praying.

Certain monks of great wisdom and deep spirituality are called lamas. They are believed to be reincarnations of great lamas who lived before them. The highest lamas embody the spirits of deities and spiritual protectors. The Dalai Lama—the spiritual leader of Tibet—is honored as a manifestation of Chenresi, the bodhisattva of compassion. The deity Amitabha is manifested in successive Panchen Lamas. Reincarnate lamas are often addressed as *Rinpoche,* meaning "Precious One" or "Cherished One."

Tibetans believe that lamas can choose the time and place of their rebirth. When such a lama dies, his reincarnation is expected within a few years.

To locate a lama's reincarnation, a group of monks form a kind of search party. They may spend years looking for signs that the lama's spirit has returned. Clues may arise in visions seen in the waters of the sacred lake Lhamo Lhatso, believed to reflect supernatural truths. They may consult the Nechung Oracle, Tibet's state oracle, who now resides in Dharamsala, India.

When the search has narrowed down to a group of candidates, they are tested. In one important test, they are shown a group of objects to see if they pick out those that were the deceased's personal possessions. Many separate tests are performed before all doubt is removed and the joyful announcement is made. The

A Tibetan artist living at Dharamsala in India paints a thangka for hanging in a temple.

child then begins years of study so that he can live up to the virtues of his former self.

Chinese government officials insist that they must confirm any selection of a reincarnated Tibetan lama. This would enable them to control the young lama's upbringing and, through him, control devout Buddhists. They are especially interested in the Panchen Lama, who is second only to the Dalai Lama.

TRADITIONAL ARTS AND CRAFTS

Thangkas are Tibet's traditional cloth paintings. Rendered on cotton cloth with a thin rod at the top, they portray Buddhist deities or themes in spectacular colors and intricate detail. Although thangkas are sold as art, Tibetan Buddhists use them as an aid to meditation. For ceremonial occasions, huge thangkas may be hung on the outside of a temple or stupa (shrine tower).

A relaxed carpet merchant in the Barkhor area of Lhasa sleeps while waiting for customers for his hand-knotted rugs.

Tibetans make metal sculptures of buddhas and other deities. Some are coated with a gold paste and studded with turquoise or coral. Artisans also make various religious objects used in rituals or to adorn temple altars. Many are made of precious metals and encrusted with gems.

Tibetans wear amulet cases called *gau*. Made of ornate silver filigree, they contain prayer scrolls, tiny statues, or charms. Gau are made in Derge, in eastern Tibet, famous for its metalwork.

Hand-knotted wool carpets are an ancient Tibetan tradition. The wool is sheared from sheep on the high Tibetan Plateau and hand-spun. Vegetable dyes produce brilliant colors of yarn, which is woven into traditional motifs, symbols, and designs.

Other traditional handcrafted items are textile goods, yak-hide saddles and shoes, pottery, and wood carvings. Today, many of these items are not authentic Tibetan designs and styles because traditional artisans no longer train apprentices.

A monk studies a Buddhist text written and bound in traditional horizontal form.

LITERATURE

Gesar, the Tibetan national epic of literature, recounts the adventures of the legendary national hero, King Gesar. With two to three million verses, it is the longest epic known. For centuries, storytellers passed on their memorized verses to younger people. Even today, there are Tibetans who can recite hundreds of thousands of verses of *Gesar*.

Tibet's major works of written literature are Buddhist texts translated from Sanskrit in the twelfth and thirteenth centuries. The 108-volume *Kangyur* recounts the words of the historical Buddha, and the 227-volume *Tengyur* contains scholars' commentaries on the *Kangyur*. Other Tibetan classics are the *Hundred Thousand Songs* of Milarepa, by a twelfth-century poet-saint, and the *Tibetan Book of the Dead*, attributed to the seventh-century mystic, Padmasambhava.

Scholarly monks produced treatises on philosophy, medicine, and astrology. They wrote manuals on practical arts such as

These special scroll trumpets are among the many musical instruments used in Tibet's ceremonies and festivals.

architecture and weapon-making. Popular literature included religious dramas, saints' biographies, and fantastic tales of warring gods and demons.

Traditional Tibetan books are packets of long, horizontal pages wrapped together. The front and back covers are wood panels. In some books, small holes are driven through one edge, and a cord is strung through and tied to hold it together. Monasteries printed books on printing presses, with the text pages on wood blocks.

It has been estimated that the Chinese destroyed 60 percent of Tibet's literature. Many of Tibet's literary treasures still exist in the minds of monks who have memorized them.

PERFORMING ARTS

Tibet's sacred music and dance are highly developed arts. Some instruments used in sacred music are Himalayan long horns *(dungchen)*, thigh-bone trumpets *(kangling)*, silver trumpets *(gyaling)*, conch shells, oboes, finger cymbals, bells, and drums.

Monks use distinctive vocal techniques in chanting. One is the Awesome Voice—a deep, reverberating tone in the lowest range of the human voice. Its vibrations envelop the listener, inducing a

A masked cham dancer performs at the Dancing Ghost Festival.

sense of the infinite. Another technique is multiphonic singing, in which a monk intones two or three notes of a chord at once.

Monks perform ceremonial dances that dramatize principles, such as the Wheel of Time, or historical events, such as the slaying of an evil king. Ritual dance called *cham* is a feature of many Tibetan festivals. The cham dancers wear masks of animals or spirits to act out religious dramas.

Tibet also has a long tradition of secular music. There were rhythmic work songs to accompany everyday labor, popular songs with hidden jabs at oppressors, and love songs. Wandering minstrels roamed the countryside and played at festivals. They accompanied their songs with native six-stringed guitars or two-stringed violins.

THE CALENDAR

The Tibetan calendar breaks time into sixty-year cycles. Each year is matched with one of five elements: iron, water, wood, fire, or earth. Each of these elements rules for two successive years—a masculine year, followed by a feminine year. In addition, each year is paired with one of twelve animals: monkey, rooster, dog, pig, mouse, ox, tiger, hare, dragon, snake, horse, and sheep. It takes sixty years to complete the cycle of ten element years paired with twelve animal years. The year 1997 on the Gregorian calendar is Tibetan year 2124, a Fire-Ox year.

Months are figured on lunar (moon) cycles, so the dates of annual festivals change slightly from year to year. The New Year begins, usually, with February's full moon. Thus the months of the Tibetan year are about six weeks later than months in the Gregorian calendar. From time to time, extra days are added, left out, or repeated in a calendar year. This adjustment makes up for the difference between a lunar year (twelve lunar months) and the solar year (365 days).

FESTIVALS AND HOLIDAYS

Traditionally, Tibetans celebrated festivals throughout the year. Public religious displays were banned in 1959 and allowed again on a limited basis in 1985. The Chinese added political holidays to the calendar as well.

In February, Tibetans all over the world celebrate Losar, the New Year festival. People dress up in their finest clothes and make early-morning incense offerings at temples, shrines, and monasteries. The streets of Lhasa throng with pilgrims. For Losar, monks perform a spectacular dance-drama to drive out the evils of the old year and bring in good luck for the year to come.

Three days after New Year, the Great Prayer Festival (Mönlam) begins. It celebrates Buddha's victory over his enemies. Huge yak-butter sculptures are put up in front of Lhasa's Jokhang Temple. Crowds of pilgrims and monks gather in the temple's Barkhor area as an image of Maitreya, the buddha yet to come, is carried in procession. Tibetans had celebrated Mönlam since Tsong Khapa instituted it in the 1400s. In 1986, they were able to observe the feast for the first time since 1959.

The full moon of the fourth month (around May) is time for Sakadawa, or Buddha's Anniversary Festival. The faithful gather at monasteries and temples to celebrate Sakyamuni's (Buddha's) birth, enlightenment, and death. A several-story-high thangka of Sakyamuni is often hung from the rooftop.

In the fifth month, usually in late June, is the Incense Festival. Being happy is the best way to observe this feast. It is the time when evil spirits are thought to be roaming around looking for unhappy souls to possess. In the sixth month, pilgrims climb holy mountains for Chökor Düchen, honoring Buddha's first sermon.

The Yogurt Festival (Shötun), at the beginning of the seventh month, begins at Drepung Monastery and proceeds to Lhasa's Norbulingka Palace. Dramas and masked dances add to the festivities. Shortly afterward is the Bathing Festival, when people

Masked monks perform a ritual dance at the annual Butter Festival ending the New Year celebrations.

A public festival in Gyantse takes place beneath a gigantic thangka.

wash themselves and their clothes in the rivers. Legends tell that this cures afflictions and disease.

The ninth month brings Lhabab Düchen, when pilgrims remember Buddha's return from heaven after teaching his mother. Yak-butter lamps flicker from windows and rooftops for the anniversary of Tsong Khapa's death in the tenth month.

At the end of the twelfth lunar month (usually late January) is the Year-End Festival, or Festival to Banish Evil Spirits. Masked monks perform ritual dances to gather up all the year's evil spirits and cast them away.

Yumbu Lakang near Tsetang was the home of the Yarlung kings.

Chapter 6

A BUDDHIST KINGDOM

According to a Buddhist creation myth, violent rainstorms in the cosmic void created a primal ocean. Rains churned the waters until the earth's dry land emerged, as butter rises from churned milk. Another myth explains the origin of the Tibetan people. Chenresi—the lord of compassion—came to earth in the form of a monkey at Tsetang, in the Yarlung Valley southeast of Lhasa. There he took compassion on a weeping ogress, and together they had six children, the ancestors of six Tibetan tribes.

Actually, not much is known about the origins of Tibetan people. Their earliest known ancestors were nomadic tribes of central Asia who migrated into Tibet's plains and river valleys.

In the early twentieth century, archeologists made a fantastic discovery in a cave in Dunhuang, in China's Gansu province. There they found a library of twenty thousand documents, dating from the fifth through the tenth centuries A.D. Buddhist monks had sealed up the cave in the year 1015. Because Dunhuang was once a part of Tibet, these records reveal many concrete details of early Tibetan history.

Other information comes from royal decrees carved on stone pillars and chronicles written during China's tenth-century T'ang dynasty. Early Buddhist writings offer some historical clues, although they mix fact with religious legend. Royal burial mounds, if they are excavated, may fill in more details.

THE FIRST YARLUNG KINGS

According to legend, Nyatri Tsenpo, the first Tibetan king, descended from heaven on a sky cord. He landed near Tsetang in the Yarlung Valley. At the end of his life, he ascended back up the cord again. His successors came and went in the same way, until the sixth king was slain by a mortal. Since then, Tibet's kings have had to live and die upon the earth.

Chieftains of the Yarlung Valley tribes were, in fact, Tibet's earliest kings. Although Nyatri Tsenpo probably did not dangle from heaven on a string, historians are able to place him in roughly the fifth century B.C. Tibetan chronicles list him as number one in a long succession of Yarlung Valley kings.

Namri Songtsen was the thirty-second king. A Yarlung tribal chief who lived from about A.D. 570 to 619, he subdued rival chiefs in the valley and took control of central Tibet. He then moved eastward to conquer tribes along the Chinese border. China's Sui Dynasty called him the Commander of 100,000 Warriors.

SONGTSEN GAMPO

It was Namri's son, Songtsen Gampo (c. 608-650), who molded Tibet into a powerful empire. By the end of his reign, his domain covered not only Tibet, but also parts of India, Nepal, Sikkim, Bhutan, and China.

To seal alliances with Nepal and China, Songtsen married the Nepalese princess Bhrikuti and the Chinese princess Wencheng. Both were Buddhists, and their faith converted the king. For all his military might, Songtsen Gampo is best known and loved as

The ornate roof of Jokhang Temple in Lhasa, seen against storm clouds, is one of the glories built by Songtsen Gampo.

the one who made Tibet a Buddhist state. He is called Tibet's First Religious King.

Songtsen Gampo moved his capital to Lhasa, where he built the Jokhang and Ramoche temples. He sent his minister, Thonmi Sambhota, to India to devise a Tibetan alphabet and script that would be suitable for translating Buddhist scriptures from Sanskrit into Tibetan. Thonmi Sambhota then began the great task of translation. Songtsen's code of law was also put into writing.

Trisong Detsen, called the Second Religious King, took the Yarlung throne in 755. He invited Buddhist scholars from India and China to come and teach in Tibet. Greatest among them were the Indian Buddhist masters Santarakshita and Padmasambhava,

Left: A pilgrim receives news from a paper written in Tibetan script,
which was developed fourteen hundred years ago under Songtsen Gampo.
Right. Pilgrims wait to enter Jokhang Temple.

also called Guru Rinpoche. With Trisong Detsen's backing, they founded Samye, Tibet's first monastery and university.

Santarakshita, as Samye's abbot, ordained Tibet's first monks there. They labored at translating volumes of Buddhist texts from Sanskrit and Chinese into Tibetan. After a great debate staged at the monastery, India's style of Buddhism was adopted over China's Zen version. Padmasambhava, adept at the mystical ways of tantrism, was brought in to combat the demons of the Bön religion. With his vibrant personality and sorcery skills, he beat the Bön priests at their wizardry.

The Third Religious King, Ralpachen, made peace with China in 821. In front of Jokhang Temple, he had the peace treaty set in stone. That stone pillar still stands today, with both parties swearing "there shall be no warfare, no hostile invasions, and no seizure of territory. . . . Tibetans shall be happy in Tibet, and Chinese shall be happy in China."

Ralpachen, assassinated in 838, was the last religious king. His brother, Langdarma, who was fiercely anti-Buddhist, took the throne as the forty-second Yarlung king. In a frenzy of demolishing monasteries and burning books, Langdarma practically wiped Buddhism off the face of Tibet. When monks assassinated Langdarma in 842, it was the end of the Yarlung reign.

Without strong leadership in Lhasa, Tibet once again broke up into small principalities. Both chieftains and monks controlled pockets of territory.

THE BUDDHIST REVIVAL

Descendants of Langdarma set up three kingdoms in western Tibet: Purang, Rutok, and Guge. The king of Guge became a monk and took the name Yeshe Ö. He built many monasteries and stupas in Guge and invited masters from India to teach Buddhism there. The greatest of these masters was the renowned Buddhist scholar Atisha, who arrived in 1042.

According to legend, Yeshe Ö paid dearly to bring Atisha to Guge. Turkic invaders captured Yeshe Ö and demanded a ransom of his weight in gold. The ransom was raised, but Yeshe Ö directed that the money be used to bring Atisha to Guge instead of rescuing him.

Atisha made Guge's monastery a great center of Buddhist learning. Beyond Guge, he inspired a revival in religious study throughout Tibet. Many of Tibet's most influential monasteries were built during this time. This period is sometimes called the "second diffusion of the doctrine" in Tibet.

Communities of monks focused on different aspects of Buddhist doctrine. This led to the formation of various orders, or sects, of Buddhism. The oldest was the Nyingmapa, or "Ancient Ones," founded by Padmasambhava in the eighth century. The Kagyupa sect originated with Marpa, a scholar who lived at the same time as Atisha. The Nyingmapa and Kaguyupa sects were sometimes called "Red Hats." Marpa's most famous student was the poet Milarepa. One of their students, Gampopa, founded the Karmapa order, a sub-sect of the Kagyupa. The Sakyapa sect was founded in 1073 at Sakya Monastery, southwest of Shigatse. It was to be the most influential sect in the years to come.

MONGOL OVERLORDS

A threat from the north pulled Tibet together again in the thirteenth century. The Mongols, under conqueror Genghis Khan, swept across central Asia and invaded western China and northern Tibet. Genghis's grandson, Godan, eventually reached to within 50 miles (80 kilometers) of Lhasa.

Godan invited Sakya Pandita, abbot of Sakya Monastery, to meet with him in 1247. Godan was so moved by Sakya Pandita's holiness that he made the monk viceroy—the king's representative—over Tibet. Thus began the patron-priest relationship (called *yoncho*) between emperor and lama that was to last for more than a century.

Godan's son, Kublai Khan, deepened the bond. He gave Sakya

Genghis Khan, the Mongol conqueror, little dreamed that his own great-grandson would convert his entire empire to Buddhism.

Pandita's nephew, Phagpa, the title of Imperial Preceptor (ruler) over Tibet. Kublai Khan promised peace and protection for Tibet. He himself converted to Buddhism in 1270 and made it the official religion of the entire Mongol empire. With so much political power in the hands of the Sakyapa lamas, other religious sects began to get jealous.

In 1280 the Mongols conquered China, where they established the Yuan Dynasty. In time, however, the Mongols' Yuan emperors began to lose their grip on China. As their influence weakened, so did the authority of the Sakyapa lamas in Tibet. Rival sects began to challenge them.

One rising dynasty of monks were members of the Kagyupa sect. Led by a monk named Changchub Gyaltsen, the members of the sect actually fought the Sakyapas and defeated them in 1354. This ended the rule of the Sakyapa order. Changchub Gyaltsen and his eleven successors ruled Tibet as both spiritual

This mountainside village lies in the Sakya Valley, southwest of Shigatse, near the monastery which, for a time, supplied the rulers of all Tibet.

and secular leaders for the next eighty years.

The Chinese overthrew the Mongols in 1368. Finally free of outside rule, China put an emperor of its own in place, establishing the Ming Dynasty. The vast Mongol empire then broke up into several smaller Mongol kingdoms scattered around central Asia, each with its own chieftain. This was the end of the important patron-priest relationship between China's Mongol rulers and Tibet's lamas.

Changchub Gyaltsen tried to wipe out all traces of the Mongols and make the country truly Tibetan. All court officials had to wear the traditional garb of the Yarlung kings' royal court. He set up a new tax system and put a new version of King Songtsen Gampo's code of laws in force. New literature emerged glorifying the grandeur of Tibet's Yarlung Kingdom and renewing its spiritual traditions.

Chapter 7

THE RULE OF
THE DALAI LAMAS

Without its Mongol overlords, Tibet faced two levels of power struggle. First, rival sects were scuffling to be the ruling monastic order. And second, nobles of central Tibet were clashing over which would dominate the others.

THE GELUKPA SECT

A boy named Tsong Khapa was born in the Kokonor region of eastern Tibet in 1357. At seventeen, he left home to study in Lhasa. He was a brilliant scholar who impressed both teachers and fellow students. Tsong Khapa was opposed to the political intrigue and loose moral values among some groups of monks. Inspired by the eleventh-

A monk at Ganden Monastery, founded by Tsong Khapa

Lhasa's Potala Palace, started by Songtsen Gampo and expanded by the "Great Fifth" Dalai Lama, stands under a rainbow. The palace is visible from many miles away.

century master Atisha, he stressed pure doctrine, strict discipline, and good moral conduct. In 1409 he founded Ganden Monastery, dedicated to the pursuit of Buddhism according to his principles. Students were bound to intense studies of religious texts, as well as rigorous rules of virtue and conduct.

Tsong Khapa's following grew into a full-fledged sect of Buddhism. It was called the Gelukpa order ("Virtuous Ones"), also known as the "Yellow Hats." Tsong Khapa's students founded the Gelukpa monasteries of Drepung in 1416 and Sera in 1419.

Gedun Drup, Tsong Khapa's nephew, founded Tashilhunpo Monastery at Shigatse in 1445. Before he died, he promised that he would reincarnate, and he left instructions on how his followers were to find him. Gedun Gyatso, identified as the reincarnation, became the abbot of Drepung Monastery.

Butter lamps burn before the High Altar at Tashilhunpo, the monastery founded by Tsong Khapa's nephew, Gedun Drup, the first Dalai Lama.

The Kagyupa monks, who had ruled Tibet since 1354, were ousted by princes of Tsang in 1435. They became the first non-monastic rulers of Tibet in centuries. The princes ruled until 1565, followed by four Tsang kings. Holding court in Shigatse, the Tsang kings had the support of the Karma sub-sect of the Kagyupa order, centered at Tsurphu Monastery.

THE DALAI LAMAS

Sonam Gyatso, the third abbot of Drepung Monastery, emerged as a great master of the Gelukpa sect. Through his influence, the Mongol leader Altan Khan, Kublai Khan's great-great-grandson, converted to Buddhism. In 1578, Altan Khan bestowed on Sonam Gyatso the title of *Dalai Lama,* meaning "Ocean of Wisdom." The tribute was extended backward in time to Gedun Drup, who was honored as the first Dalai Lama, making Sonam Gyatso the third. Thus began the succession of Dalai Lamas that continues to this day. Today's Dalai Lama is the fourteenth.

Once again, a bond was made between a Mongol lord and a Tibetan lama—this time, a lama of the Gelukpa sect. This alliance worried the Tsang kings and their Karmapa supporters. Relations between the two sides deteriorated. It became even worse when Sonam Gyatso's reincarnation, the fourth Dalai Lama, was found to be Altan Khan's great-grandson.

Finally, in 1611, the Tsang king attacked Drepung and Sera monasteries. The twenty-year-old fourth Dalai Lama fled. He died five years later, possibly by poisoning. In 1642, Mongol warrior Gushri Khan invaded Tibet and conquered Tsang. His ally, the fifth Dalai Lama, was his partner in victory.

An immense mural at Samye Monastery shows the Great Fifth Dalai Lama, along with Sangye Gyatso, the regent of his successor.

THE GREAT FIFTH

The fifth Dalai Lama, Ngawang Lobsang Gyatso, is honored as the greatest leader in Tibet's history. He is often called simply the Great Fifth. With the military assistance of Gushri Khan, he unified Tibet from the far western kingdoms to Kham in the east.

Enthroned as Tibet's king, he was acknowledged by both Gushri Khan and the Chinese emperor as Tibet's secular leader.

The Great Fifth made Lhasa his capital. On Lhasa's Red Hill, he expanded the Potala, started by Songtsen Gampo, and turned it into his palace and fortress. To manage his kingdom, he set up a system of government that remained in place until 1959. His court of ministers and advisors consisted of monks and members of Tibet's noble families. He installed governors and other administrators throughout the kingdom to oversee the people and collect taxes.

Under the Great Fifth, the Gelukpa monasteries of Ganden, Sera, and Drepung were expanded. The Dalai Lama also renovated crumbling temples and built many new ones. He was also a brilliant scholar, writing many important treatises.

Shortly after the fifth Dalai Lama took the throne, China's Ming Dynasty fell. Once again, China was conquered by warlords from outside its borders. This time the conquerors were the Manchus, from the Manchuria region northeast of China. In 1644, the Manchus established the Qing Dynasty in China.

The Great Fifth died in 1682. A young boy was put in place as the sixth Dalai Lama, while his regent, Sangye Gyatso, ruled Tibet. Amazingly, the regent kept the Great Fifth's death a secret from the Chinese for thirteen years. He told them that the Dalai Lama had gone into a long period of meditation.

MANCHUS VERSUS MONGOLS

The sixth Dalai Lama proved to be a weak leader. This made Tibet an easy target for both Mongols and Manchus, who had become the two superpowers in central Asia. China's Manchu

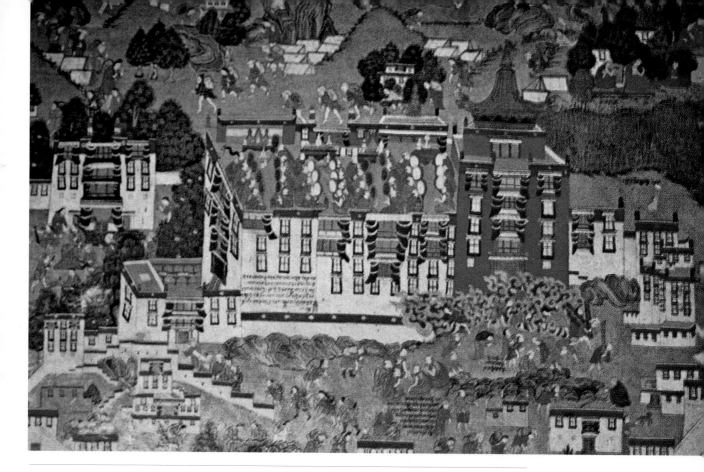

A mural at Potala Palace records the beginning of construction of the great 1,200-room palace in Lhasa.

emperor Kangxi encouraged a Mongol prince, Lhabzang Khan, to invade Tibet in 1706 and murder the regent. The sixth Dalai Lama also died under mysterious circumstances, and Lhabzang put a substitute in his place. Another band of Mongols, angry over the Dalai Lama's death, attacked Lhasa in 1717 and killed Lhabzang.

This invasion gave Emperor Kangxi a perfect opportunity to march an army into Tibet. He drove the Mongols out, enthroned the seventh Dalai Lama, and declared Tibet a protectorate of China. By 1720, he had Manchu troops stationed in Lhasa and two

Manchu representatives *(ambans)* in the Dalai Lama's court.

Since Dalai Lamas were chosen as children, their regents sometimes spent many years ruling in their name. After the seventh Dalai Lama died in 1757, the post of regent was made an official government position, to be held only by one of the few monks given the title of *lama*. The ninth through the twelfth Dalai Lamas all died before they were old enough to rule. One regent after another governed Tibet until the late 1800s.

Gurkha warriors from Nepal invaded Tibet in 1788, and China helped repel them. After that, Tibet was closed to foreigners. That was also the last time that the Manchus were involved in Tibet's foreign affairs.

For the next century, the Manchus were occupied with problems at home. From 1839 to 1842, China and Great Britain clashed in what was called the Opium War. Next, they were faced with the long-drawn-out Taiping Rebellion (1850 to 1864) against Manchu rule in China.

Meanwhile, Tibet had its own battles to fight. On its western front, Tibet fought with the kingdom of Jammu (now a part of India) from 1841 to 1842. From 1854 to 1855, there were skirmishes with Nepal again. Tibet entered into peace treaties with both opponents. Its next foe would be Great Britain.

THE GREAT GAME

India at this time was a colony of Great Britain. Britain wanted to open up Tibet for trade, but Tibet refused to discuss the matter. Meanwhile, Britain was engaged in a power struggle with Russia, to the north of Tibet and China. The British saw their conflict as

As Britain added Tibet to its Great Game, British artists gave the public their impressions of life in Tibet.

sort of a sport, which they called the Great Game.

Britain was afraid that Russia had its eye on Tibet. Rumors began flying around British India that Tibet and Russia were on the verge of making a deal. The British decided to prevent that happening.

Colonel Francis Younghusband led British troops into Tibet in 1903. The thirteenth Dalai Lama, twenty-seven years old, fled to safety in Mongolia. Younghusband took Lhasa by killing six hundred Tibetans, who were armed with only knives and primitive rifles. The Dalai Lama returned in 1907, and Britain and Tibet opened trade relations.

In 1910 Lhasa was again invaded, this time by the Manchus. The Dalai Lama fled to India, under British protection. In 1911, China's Republican Revolution toppled the Manchus' Qing Dynasty. Over the next year, Tibetans expelled the Manchu troops, as well as the two Manchu ambans at the Dalai Lama's court. The Dalai Lama returned in 1913 to rule what had finally become a purely Tibetan nation.

THE THIRTEENTH DALAI LAMA MODERNIZES

The thirteenth Dalai Lama, Thupten Gyatso, was Tibet's greatest reformer since the Great Fifth in the seventeenth century. He realized that Tibet was badly in need of an overhaul. Experience had shown that Tibet could not defend itself very well and was not in tune with the modern world.

China's new president, Yuan Shikai, hoped to keep a grip on Tibet and be friends at the same time. He sent the Dalai Lama a message apologizing for the Manchus and offering to let him keep his position as Dalai Lama.

The Dalai Lama replied that he already was the Dalai Lama. He further stated that he was not interested in any honors from China and that he was busy taking care of his country's affairs. Tibet declared its independence, then proceeded to fly its own flag and to issue its own money, passports, and stamps.

The British organized the Simla Conference in 1913. They hoped to arrange an agreement that spelled out the relationship between Tibet and China. China, however, refused to sign it. This left many unresolved issues, such as where the China–Tibet border lay. The Chinese had already taken over part of Tibet's Amdo and Kham provinces. At the conference, the British, at least, recognized Tibet's independence by setting the India–Tibet border.

With the help of the British, the Dalai Lama organized an army with modern weapons and training. He had telegraph lines

The thirteenth Dalai Lama, Thupten Gyatso, shown here in 1930 seated on his Lion Throne, was responsible for considerable modernization in Tibet.

strung, built a hydroelectric plant near Lhasa, and opened an English school at Gyantse. Selected Tibetan students were sent to England to study.

Perhaps his biggest challenge was to reform the way the government worked. Tibet had been organized in a feudal system,

Villagers, such as these in the Sakya Valley, were long under the control of the local monastery, which owned all the land. The thirteenth Dalai Lama tried to reform Tibet, so that peasants could own their own land, but many monastery officials were reluctant to let go of it.

with most of the farmland belonged to huge estates. Monasteries, noble families, and government officials owned the estates. Peasants worked the land as serfs, giving a percentage of their crops to the owners.

This system worked fairly well for most Tibetans, but there was plenty of room for corruption. Estate owners—both monks and nobles—had complete authority over their serfs. Some demanded exorbitant taxes and grain payments, leaving their serfs with barely enough to stay alive.

The Dalai Lama set out to clean up the system. He reformed the feudal laws so that peasants were able to own land themselves. He also changed the tax system so that common people would have a chance to prosper. He banned brutal punishments and got rid of dozens of corrupt officials.

These changes were too drastic to take effect peacefully. Monks resisted losing power and feared the rising influence of non-monks. They saw the secular army as a challenge to the monasteries' own monk-soldiers. Under pressure from conservatives, the army and the police force were reduced and some of the British-led modernizations were dismantled. A dispute arose between the Lhasa government and the Panchen Lama over taxation of monasteries, and the Panchen Lama left for China.

In 1933 the thirteenth Dalai Lama died. He had spent twenty years trying to modernize Tibet, but it was too short a time. Transportation and communications were still primitive, and peasants' lives were still backward in many ways. The Chinese had been a constant problem. In border battles throughout the 1920s, they had annexed even more of Amdo and Kham.

The Dalai Lama may have foreseen what horrors lay ahead for Tibet. Before his death, he prophesied that Tibetans' way of life was going to be destroyed. A time would come, he said, when all lamas would die and no searches would be permitted for their successors. Tibetans would starve and live in fear, and not a vestige would be left of their ancient wisdom and culture.

India won its independence from Great Britain in 1947. The British then pulled their advisors out of Tibet. Without Britain on the scene, China could move on Tibet without fear of a powerful opponent. Sadly, China's next attempt on Tibet would succeed.

Above: In October 1950, the Chinese People's Liberation Army drove into Tibet "to liberate the Tibetans and safeguard the frontiers of China."

Left: Since the takeover of Tibet by China, many Chinese families have moved into Tibet. This child will grow up with her culture imposed on Tibetan society.

Chapter 8

TIBET UNDER CHINA

Mao Zedong and his Chinese Communist Party overthrew the Nationalist Chinese government in 1949. Mao named his new, revolutionary nation the People's Republic of China, with himself as Communist Party chairman and president.

For Tibet, with its Buddhist outlook, no one could have seemed more alien than Mao. He taught that religion is a poison that keeps people ignorant. Power, said Mao, comes from the barrel of a gun. He lost no time wielding that power in Tibet.

CHINESE INVASION

In October 1950, Mao's People's Liberation Army began a full-scale invasion of Tibet. Thirty thousand Chinese troops came in from six directions. From the east, troops marched into Tibet's Kham province and captured the city of Chamdo.

Ordinarily, a Dalai Lama assumes his position as head of state at age eighteen. Because of the national crisis, Tibet's government called for an early enthronement. Thus, at the age of sixteen, the fourteenth Dalai Lama began his reign.

In May 1951, China presented Tibet with a seventeen-point plan for the "peaceful liberation of Tibet." Under this agreement, China would be in charge of Tibet's military and foreign affairs. It would build roads, schools, and hospitals and create new industries. Tibet would keep its language and religious freedom but would give up political independence.

The Dalai Lama's government appealed to the United Nations for help but got no support. Some Tibetans thought the arrangement might not be too bad for them. Having no other choice, Tibet agreed to be "liberated."

Throughout the country, however, armed resistance to Chinese occupation seethed. Guerrilla fighters ambushed Chinese camps in central and eastern Tibet. But without a modern army, the Tibetans could not hold back Chinese advances. Piece by piece, China annexed more of Tibet. The Chinese reached Lhasa in September 1951 and began Tibet's "peaceful liberation" in earnest.

Massive construction projects got underway to build roads and power plants. The new roads turned out to be good military supply lines. Hundreds of ballistic missiles were brought in from China and set up along Tibet's borders. The "re-education" of the Tibetan people began, too. That is, they could pledge loyalty to the Chinese Communist system or be beaten.

In 1956 Khampa tribesmen in eastern Tibet broke into outright rebellion. Monks in the region joined them. Thousands of monks defended Litang Monastery against a siege. But they were no match for Chinese aerial bombs.

LHASA UPRISING

Lhasa was packed with refugees and pilgrims for the New Year festival in 1959. The streets were thick with armed Chinese guards, too. The Dalai Lama received an invitation to watch a dance performance at the Chinese military base. It was worded

As the Lhasa uprising failed, the Dalai Lama, guarded by Khampa tribesmen, escaped into India with his family.

in such a way that he could not refuse. Also, he was not to bring his usual contingent of bodyguards.

News of the invitation leaked out into the streets of Lhasa. Tibetans were sure the Chinese meant to kidnap or kill the Dalai Lama. Fearful for their leader's life, people swarmed in front of his residence, the Norbulingka Palace. The Chinese began arming themselves for battle, and Tibet's government ministers declared all deals with China null and void.

The Dalai Lama's pleas for calm were answered with mortar fire. He realized the chances for peaceful compromise were over. Disguised as a soldier, he slipped out of the palace in the dead of night. Along with family members and supporters, he fled across the mountains into India, with fierce and loyal Khampa tribesmen as his escorts and guards.

Left: In the shadow of the Dalai Lama's Potala Palace, Chinese officials read an edict that clamped their control of the Tibetan people even tighter. Above: The Chinese quickly destroyed thousands of monasteries, declaring religious practice illegal.

Chinese artillery wrecked Norbulingka Palace. Soldiers sorted through the debris to confirm the Dalai Lama's death, only to discover that he had escaped. An all-out battle began. Sick of Chinese occupation, Tibetans fought wildly for three days. The Chinese shelled not only Norbulingka, but also the Potala Palace, Sera Monastery, and the Medical College. Thousands of people huddled in Jokhang Temple for refuge, but it, too, was bombed.

Once the dust had settled, the streets of Lhasa were littered with bodies. Chinese radio broadcasts proclaimed the body count to be eighty thousand.

"DEMOCRATIC REFORMS"

After the Lhasa uprising failed, a mass exodus began. It was a sorry affair. Most fleeing Tibetans hoped to escape across the treacherous Himalayas into India, Nepal, or Bhutan. But Chinese armed guards were stationed at the mountain passes, and many Tibetans were killed in flight. Others froze or starved as they fled. Some guides offered safe passage to refugees for a fee, then turned them in to the Chinese for a second fee. Of the six thousand monks in Drepung Monastery, only a couple of hundred succeeded in escaping into India.

Thousands of refugees made their way to northern India, where the Dalai Lama had settled. There he and his supporters set up a Tibetan government-in-exile. They planned to continue their job of overseeing the Tibetan people, even if they had to do it from outside Tibet.

China then launched what it called "democratic reforms" in Tibet. Chinese officials disbanded Tibet's government and confiscated all lands from monasteries and upper-class Tibetans. More than six thousand monasteries, some of them over a thousand years old, were demolished. Shelling them was a war game, useful for artillery practice. Monks were herded into prison camps and put to work on construction crews. Precious artworks, centuries old, were sold to art dealers in Hong Kong and Japan. Gold and silver religious objects were melted down, and ancient manuscripts were burned. Religious practice was banned.

Many thousands of Chinese people were relocated to work on Tibet's farms and construction sites. This helped relieve China's overpopulation problem, but it did more than that. As the migrations increased, Tibetans in many regions found themselves outnumbered. Chinese men were encouraged to marry Tibetan women and to raise their children speaking only Chinese. Clearly, China was trying to wipe out Tibetans as a people.

Farmland was redistributed, and agriculture was organized

Tibetan farmers were organized by the Chinese into communes. These commune-owned trucks are heading to fields in the Shigatse region.

into communes. Instead of their traditional barley, Tibetan farmers were told to raise wheat and rice. But Tibet's climate was unsuitable for the new crops. When crops failed and famine swept the land, thousands died of starvation.

The eastern forests were stripped bare to supply wood for construction projects. Beautiful animals, some of them rare, were slaughtered to feed the Chinese army. Herds of antelopes and wild yaks were machined-gunned, and songbirds were blasted out of trees. Golden-haired Lhasa Apso dogs, favorite pets of the upper class, were shot out of contempt for their former owners.

A NATION AMONG NATIONS

The Chinese justified their invasion by claiming that Tibet was already theirs—that Tibet had been a Chinese territory for hundreds of years. To the Dalai Lama, Tibet's status as a sovereign nation was an important point. After his escape, he appealed to the International Commission of Jurists to review Tibet's situation. The court ruled that from 1913 to 1950 Tibet had functioned in every way as an independent, sovereign state. It had conducted its own foreign and domestic affairs and entered into treaties with other nations. The court absolutely debunked China's claims on Tibet and condemned the invasion.

Unfortunately, this ruling did not muster any real international support for Tibet. Later in 1959, the issue of Tibet came before the United Nations. Communist countries, led by Russia, took China's side. India and Great Britain took the position that the situation in Tibet was unclear. In the end, a mild resolution was passed calling for human rights for Tibetans.

The Panchen Lama, second in authority to the Dalai Lama, was only eleven years old when China invaded Tibet. As he got older, he believed he could work with the Chinese in making a better life for Tibetans. By 1964, he had winessed so much pitiful devastation in his homeland that he publicly denounced China. For this he was sent to a Chinese prison for ten years.

In September 1965, with much fanfare, China officially established the Tibet Autonomous Region. ·The saddest chapter in Tibet's history was about to begin.

CULTURAL REVOLUTION

Mao Zedong imposed his Cultural Revolution on Tibet in 1966. Mao's Red Guards, with their young Tibetan recruits, set to work with revolutionary zeal. Their mission was to wipe out the "four olds"—old thought, old culture, old habits, and old customs.

The Dalai Lama was declared an "enemy of the people." Tibetans were compelled to renounce him, and anyone who was found to have his picture was sent to jail. Any opposition was cruelly crushed. Monks and nuns, who often were the ones to protest, were imprisoned, tortured, or executed. Many people were shot in plain sight of others to serve as examples. Others were simply stomped to death in dark alleys. Entire villages were destroyed, and the villagers crucified or hung.

Workers were taught Mao's Communist principles. Anyone who failed to have the proper attitude was subjected to "struggle sessions"—torture sessions, really—that were sometimes fatal.

As in its other provinces, China enforced a strict policy of population control. Women and young girls were forcibly sterilized, and pregnant women were given abortions. One Tibetan doctor in a Lhasa hospital reported witnessing fifty to sixty abortions a week, as well as the killing of infants by lethal injection. These were ways China used to solve what it called Tibet's "ethnic problem."

According to China, everyone was thriving and happy. "The peaceful liberation of Tibet," said a Chinese publication, "gave the region a new lease on life. . . . Since then, the once downtrodden masses have led a free, happy life."

BITTEN BY A SNAKE

After Mao died in 1976, his successors relaxed some of the restrictions in Tibet. They released the Panchen Lama from prison and even invited the Dalai Lama to return. But, as the Dalai Lama said, "Once bitten by a snake, you feel suspicious even when you see a piece of rope." Instead, he sent a series of fact-finding

Left: In 1979, young Tibetan students were overlooked by photos of Chinese officials. Above: A 1,000-room tourist hotel was built in Lhasa to celebrate the TAR's twentieth anniversary in 1985, but no tourists were allowed.

delegations into Tibet. They found the place a shambles. It was estimated that 1.2 million people had died since the Chinese takeover through executions, torture, imprisonment, and starvation.

Meanwhile, other countries had been pressuring China to ease up on Tibet. China's new leader, Deng Xiaoping, sent his own observers into Tibet in 1980. They realized that the big experiment in Tibet had failed. Over the next few years, many changes were made. Farming communes were disbanded, and people returned to their traditional crops and farming methods.

In September 1985, China held a great celebration in Lhasa to honor the twentieth anniversary of the Tibet Autonomous Region. Several shiny new buildings were built in Lhasa for the occasion. Chinese officials proudly passed out souvenirs, electronic clocks, and tea bags.

Tibetans were given back some of their religious freedoms in 1985. Reconstruction began on a few monasteries, and a limited number of people were allowed to study to become monks and nuns. People were allowed to practice their religion in public once again, though in a smaller, quieter way than before.

STILL NOT HAPPY, STILL NOT FREE

In spite of the reforms, Tibetans were far from "happy and free." In September 1987, monks in Lhasa staged a pro-independence demonstration. By the time the protests ended nine days later, several people had been killed. Lhasa's Drapchi prison was filled with arrested monks. Demonstrations during a religious festival in March 1988 led to several deaths and more arrests.

The Dalai Lama then made a new proposal to China. Instead of giving Tibet complete independence, he suggested, let Tibet become a self-governing Chinese territory. Tibet would manage its domestic affairs, and China would handle foreign affairs and the military. Chinese officials refused to discuss the idea.

After years in prison, the Panchen Lama was supposed to be "rehabilitated," meaning that he had become pro-Chinese. However, in January 1989, he flatly stated that Tibetans had paid too high a price for their modernization. A few days later he was dead. The official cause of death was a heart attack, but many people suspect he had been poisoned.

In March 1989, the thirtieth anniversary of the Lhasa uprising, pro-independence riots erupted again. Sixteen protesters were killed. Many Buddhist nuns who took part in the demonstrations were cruelly tortured. For the first time since 1959, Lhasa was put

Tibetans at Nechung Monastery pray using their personal prayer wheels. Perhaps they are silently praying for the release of political prisoners.

under martial law. During the next year, an estimated two thousand people were executed.

In October 1989, the Dalai Lama was awarded the Nobel Peace Prize for his commitment to nonviolence and world peace. China denounced the prize committee, saying it was trying to meddle in China's internal affairs.

Again in 1990 and 1993, the Dalai Lama proposed a compromise with China but to no avail. Meanwhile, demonstrations and bloodshed continued, with major outbreaks in October 1991, March 1992, and May 1993. The Dalai Lama began to realize, as he had in 1959, that the chances for a peaceful compromise were slim.

THE STRUGGLE CONTINUES

In 1995, the Dalai Lama named a six-year-old boy from a remote nomad region of Tibet as the Panchen Lama's reincarnation. Chinese officials angrily rejected the Dalai Lama's choice. They said that his methods were illegal and that the boy was a fraud. The boy was taken into custody in Beijing, and China

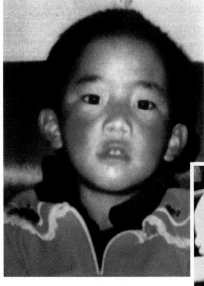

In 1995 the Dalai Lama chose six-year-old Gedun Choekyi Nyima (left) to be the eleventh Panchen Lama. Chinese officials quickly replaced him with the boy below.

engineered its own search. "No Tibetan will be fooled by this," commented Lodi Gyari, the Dalai Lama's representative.

Other events in 1995 focused world attention on Tibet. Seven Tibetans staged a hunger strike in New York City during the United Nations's fiftieth anniversary celebrations. Phuntsok Nyidron, a 27-year-old nun and freedom fighter in a Tibetan prison, was awarded the Reebok Human Rights Award.

Tibet continues its struggle to be free. Tourism is increasing, but visitors are tightly controlled, seeing only what the Chinese let them see. Soldiers and police roam the streets of Lhasa to stop demonstrations. Plainclothes security guards mingle in crowds, watching tourists and locals alike. Undercover policemen live in monasteries, dressed as monks, to act as informants.

By the final years of the twentieth century, many of China's older officials had grown old or died. Deng Xiaoping, who had held the reins of power since 1980, lay gravely ill. Observers around the world wondered what shifts in policy his death might bring. Will new leaders open up more freedoms in China, or will they clamp down harder than before? Whatever the answer, the future of Tibet hangs in the balance.

Chapter 9

THE DALAI LAMA
AND THE EXILE

Tibetans love the Dalai Lama. They cherish him not only as their spiritual leader, but also as their secular leader who works tirelessly for their well-being. Western travelers to Tibet are often swarmed with Tibetans asking for Dalai Lama pictures.

The Dalai Lama's proper form of address is "His Holiness the Dalai Lama." Tenzin Gyatso is his name. He was born in 1935 in Amdo province, in far northeastern Tibet, not far from the present-day city of Xining.

THE SEARCH

After the thirteenth Dalai Lama died in 1933, his body was preserved and placed in the Potala Palace. High lamas began looking for signs of his reincarnation. One day, they noticed that the deceased lama's head had turned to face the east. This suggested that his return would be somewhere to the east.

The monks made visits to the sacred lake Lhamo Lhatso, where they meditated and prayed for signs. One of them saw, reflected in the lake, visions that he did not quite understand. There was a monastery with golden-peaked rooftops, a winding road leading

The fourteenth, and current, Dalai Lama was fifteen years old when the Chinese invaded Tibet.

to a hill shaped like a stupa, or Buddhist shrine. He also saw a house with turquoise-colored tiles.

In strict secrecy, several search parties of monks set out into eastern Tibet in 1937. One group came upon a scene that exactly matched the vision—the monastery with golden peaks, the winding road, the hill, and the house with the tiles. The monastery was Kumbum Monastery, which marks the birthplace of Tsong Khapa, founder of the Gelukpa order.

With the head lama disguised as a servant, the search party approached the house. Inside lived a family with a two-year-old boy. The child sprang up and ran directly to the servant, calling him by his proper title as head lama of Sera Monastery. The boy was especially interested in the lama's rosary and he grabbed for it. It had belonged to the thirteenth Dalai Lama.

It looked as if the long search might be over. The child passed all standard tests, one after the other. Once all doubt was removed, he was officially confirmed as the authentic reincarnation of the past Dalai Lama. The next step was to take the child to Lhasa, where he would begin his religious studies.

At this time, Amdo province was under the control of a local Chinese warlord. He demanded a ransom equal to about $92,000 to let the toddler go. It took two years for the monks to raise that money. Finally, in 1940, at the age of four-and-a-half, the boy was enthroned in Lhasa as the fourteenth Dalai Lama.

The Dalai Lama assumed political leadership of his country at age sixteen, but he did not take his final exams to confirm his position as the spiritual ruler of all Tibetans until he was twenty-four, after twenty years of study. These were lengthy oral exams in which Buddhist masters questioned him and engaged him in debate. Buddhist religious debate is a high art form—loud, lively, aggressive, and good-natured all at once. The opponents argue points of religion, philosophy, and metaphysics, using Buddhist scriptures to back up their claims. There are literally millions of verses of scripture on which to draw.

The Dalai Lama's final examination took place in public before the Jokhang Temple. Thousands of spectators—monks and laypeople alike—attended the day-long affair. The three-part exam covered logic in the morning, perfection of wisdom in the afternoon, and meta-physics in the evening. Eighteen of Tibet's highest Buddhist scholars grilled him with questions and wrangled in debate. The Dalai Lama proved himself in all categories and

The Dalai Lama (right) met with the leader of Sikkim just before his escape to India.

A second Nechung Monastery has been built in Dharamsala, India, the city where the Dalai Lama lives in exile.

was awarded the degree of Master of Metaphysics. Shortly after, the Chinese general in Lhasa sent the Dalai Lama the invitation that led to the bloody Lhasa uprising and his flight to India.

PLEAS AND PROPOSALS

The Dalai Lama meets with presidents and prime ministers of nations all over the world. His mission is to tell about the Tibetans' plight and to muster support for Tibet's independence. Other nations receive him with tremendous respect. However, few countries officially recognize him as Tibet's legitimate leader. They do not want to risk offending China or losing their trade agreements with this major world power.

In 1987 the Dalai Lama addressed the U.S. Congress's Human Rights Caucus on the plight of Tibet. In this speech, he outlined his Five-Point Peace Plan for Tibet. His proposed that: (1) Tibet become a demilitarized "zone of peace," (2) Chinese immigration be stopped, (3) basic human rights be restored, (4) Tibet's natural resources be protected, and (5) Tibet and China begin serious discussions about Tibet's future.

Sixty-seven members of Congress wrote to President Ronald Reagan asking him to take action on Tibet's behalf. The U.S. State Department replied that Tibet is part of China and that the U.S. does not want to risk damaging its relations with China. The Dalai Lama has subsequently met with Presidents George Bush and Bill Clinton.

GOVERNMENT-IN-EXILE

After the Dalai Lama escaped Tibet in 1959, he and his supporters settled in Dharamsala, in the Indian state of Himachal Pradesh. There they organized a Tibetan government-in-exile, complete with all the departments necessary to manage a country.

The Dalai Lama soon began restructuring the government to make it more like a parliamentary democracy. He added an Assembly of Tibetan People's Deputies, consisting of elected representatives. Today, the exile government has expanded to include a Supreme Justice Commission and eight administrative departments. Eighteen is the minimum age for voting.

Offices representing the Dalai Lama's government have been opened in major cities around the world. Among the first to open were those in New Delhi, India, and Kathmandu, Nepal. Today, offices of Tibet are also operating in New York City; London, England; Tokyo, Japan; Geneva, Switzerland; Moscow, Russia;

*The Library of Tibetan Works and Archives at Dharamsala is an
important world resource of information on Tibet.*

Budapest, Hungary; Paris, France; and Canberra, Australia. These
offices spread information on current events in Tibet, promote
Tibetan culture and arts, and help Tibetans to get settled in their
new communities.

The Department of Information and International Relations
communicates with foreign offices all over the world. Other
departments administer schools, health-care centers, and refugee
settlements in India, Nepal, and Bhutan. In the early 1990s, 92
percent of Tibetan children in these communities were in school.

The Department of Religion and Culture sponsors institutes for
Tibetan performing arts, literary works, and higher studies. It also
oversees about two hundred monasteries and convents..

Some of the institutions at Dharamsala are the Tibetan Medical
and Astro. Institute, the Library of Tibetan Works and Archives,
the Tibetan Institute of Performing Arts, and the Tibetan

Pilgrims to Dharamsala circumambulate the Dalai Lama's residence just as they would in Tibet.

Children's Village, which was first set up as a home for the thousands of orphaned children who escaped Tibet. Today, the Children's Village is also home to children who have been smuggled out of Tibet for their safety.

The Tibetan communities themselves generate about one-third of their operating costs. The rest comes from public and private contributions. The goal of the Tibetans' development plan is to become completely self-sufficient.

THE CONSTITUTION

A new constitution was drafted in 1963. Until the people of Tibet are able to cast votes on the document, it is still considered a proposal. This constitution is remarkable, as it combines a Buddhist outlook with modern issues such as conservation and nuclear warfare.

The 1963 constitution calls for executive, legislative, and judicial branches of government. The executive branch would consist of the Dalai Lama and his cabinet. The Commission of People's Deputies (now the Assembly of Tibetan People's

Deputies) would be the lawmaking, or legislative, branch. Judges of the Supreme Court would interpret the laws.

The Dalai Lama was not completely happy with this constitution. In particular, he began to feel that a Dalai Lama should not be the head of state. As he explained, "I felt that this fell short of fulfilling the requirement of a democratic system to its full extent."

He has since proposed that the Tibetan people, once they are free, elect all their leaders, including a president to be head of state and chief executive. The government-in-exile would then close down, and the Dalai Lama would be simply a monk.

AROUND THE WORLD

After the Lhasa uprising in 1959, about 80,000 Tibetan refugees escaped into India, Nepal, Bhutan, and Sikkim (now part of India). Today, about 100,000 Tibetans live in forty-six refugee settlements on the Indian subcontinent. About 15,000 live in Nepal, mostly in Kathmandu. Each of the communities has its own schools, monasteries, and medical centers.

Monks from some of Tibet's major monasteries have simply reopened their institutions in exile. Only 216 monks from Drepung Monastery escaped the Chinese crackdown. They settled in Karnataka state in southern India, where they founded a new Drepung Monastery. The newly established Sera and Ganden monasteries are also in southern India. Many distinguished monks have settled in European and American cities, where they teach and work with their communities.

Tibetan refugees and their children have settled in thirty-three countries around the world. They live in Switzerland, France,

American singer and environmental activist John Denver met with the Dalai Lama (right) at the Earth Summit in Brazil in 1992.

England, Australia, Canada, Mexico, and the United States, including Alaska. Local support groups help them with living arrangements, job placement, and cultural programs. In 1990, the U.S. Congress passed a law allowing one thousand immigrant visas to be issued to Tibetan refugees.

Current information on Tibet is available from a number of sources. The government-in-exile's Department of Information publishes the *Tibetan Bulletin,* as well as books, pamphlets, and statistical surveys on conditions in Tibet.

The International Campaign for Tibet is based in Washington, D.C. It works to promote human rights and self-determination for Tibetans and to protect their culture and environment. Tibet Information Network, based in London, England, investigates and publishes facts about human rights in Tibet. Human Rights Watch/Asia and Amnesty International also publish information on conditions in Tibet.

Above: Monks at Shalu Monastery use the old Central Hall to sleep in while they work to restore the building. Below: Shoppers in a Lhasa market ignore Tibetan pilgrims as they prostrate themselves while circumambulating Jokhang Temple.

Chapter 10

GOVERNMENT AND ECONOMY

Tibet's government until 1959 was a theocracy—it was ruled by a religious authority. The Dalai Lama was the nation's spiritual leader as well as its chief executive. Under the Dalai Lama were two prime ministers—a monk and a layman.

The Council of Ministers (the *Kashag*) was composed of four laymen. They directed home affairs, foreign affairs, the economy, and defense. About twenty government departments handled finance, revenue, and other areas. Monks in the Department of Religious Affairs oversaw the monasteries and chose monk officials.

Tibet's National Assembly had about 350 members. Sixty of its members formed the Working Committee. Recommendations of these groups went to the Dalai Lama for approval. For local rule, regional governors and district administrators oversaw about 240 districts. Most of these officials were appointed, and some inherited their positions. Each village chose a representative to deal with the central government. Nomads lived outside this system.

GOVERNMENT UNDER CHINA

The People's Republic of China is divided into twenty-three provinces, five autonomous regions, and three municipalities. The autonomous regions are set up for ethnic minorities. China established the Tibet Autonomous Region in 1965.

For governing purposes, the TAR is broken into seven prefectures (Ngari, Shigatse, Gyantse, Shannan, Nyingchi, Chamdo, and Nagchu) and one regional municipality (Lhasa). Each of these is subdivided into counties, for a total of seventy-seven counties. There are also seven "minority townships."

The Communist Party Committee and the Regional People's Congress are the governing bodies of the TAR. Both institutions have officials at the regional, district, and village levels. The Communist Party and the People's Congress also direct a number of political committees. There is also a system of People's Courts.

THE MILITARY

Between 300,000 and 500,000 Chinese troops—the People's Liberation Army (PLA)—are permanently stationed in the TAR. Their military commander lives in Lhasa. Army camps line Tibet's southern border with Nepal, India, and Bhutan. Tibetans are drafted into the PLA for army, security, and local militia duty.

China has an estimated fourteen military airfields, seventeen radar stations, and five nuclear bases in Tibet. Tibet also has one of China's largest ICBM (intercontinental ballistic missile) bases. Over one hundred long- and short-range ballistic missiles are positioned in Tibet's border regions.

China built its major nuclear weapons research facility on the Tibetan Plateau in the 1960s. It is located near Lake Kokonor in Amdo province (China's Qinghai province). Over the years, nuclear accidents and pollution have been reported at the site. At

A contemporary store in the Ngari district is stocked with Chinese goods.

times, China has imposed bans on eating fish from the lake and eating the meat of sheep that graze nearby. Several children in the area have died from unusual diseases. Area residents have reported other strange disorders.

In 1964 China conducted its first nuclear test at Lop Nor, a dry lake bed just north of the TAR's border. Tibetans were reportedly evacuated from the region after nuclear tests in 1982.

China began discussions in the 1980s with other countries about disposing of their radioactive nuclear wastes. China could collect enormous fees for taking these hazardous materials. Some observers believe that China is considering Tibet's northern plateau as a likely dumping site.

THE ECONOMY

Before 1950, agriculture was Tibet's main economic activity. Tibet exported wool, animal skins and products, medicinal herbs, borax, mica, and salt to India, Nepal, Bhutan, and China. Imports included tea, silk, and porcelain from China; textiles, sugar, rice, and fuels from India; and rice and dried fruit from Nepal and Bhutan. Among Tibetans, very little money changed hands. People bartered with each other for farm products, household goods, and other necessities.

China's economic development of Tibet has helped in some ways and hurt in others. The Chinese have invested a lot of money in Tibet. They built roads, brought in farm machinery, and developed new mining and manufacturing industries. After twenty years, however, Tibet's economy was in very poor shape.

In the mid-1980s, even Chinese economists complained that their government was spending too much on developing Tibet. They pointed out that for every yuan worth of goods and services Tibet produced, it cost China 1.2 yuan in government payments, or subsidies.

Outside of China, critics say that Tibet's modernization benefits China rather than Tibet. Workers who manage and operate Tibet's industries are Chinese, not Tibetan. Minerals, timber, and agricultural products ride on new trucks, over new roads, right to China.

The average income per person for China as a whole is equal to about $400 a year. In the TAR, the estimated annual income per person in 1990 was $80.

INDUSTRY

Before the 1950s, there were almost no mechanized industries in Tibet. After 1950, Chinese technicians set up factories and trained Tibetan workers. An ironwork factory and a woodwork

Left: Brick-making is an almost perpetual activity in Tibet.
Above: One man's open-air bicycle shop is prepared to fix almost anything, while the customer waits.

factory opened in Lhasa in 1952. A motor-vehicle repair shop opened in 1957 and a tannery the following year.

Today, the TAR's industries produce dozens of products in over two hundred small and medium-sized factories. They account for about 20 percent of the TAR's total production. Factories in the Lhasa area make machinery, textiles, carpets, chemicals, and books. Plants process leather, grain, and other farm products. As a rule, Chinese immigrants manage and operate these industries, and about half the workers are Chinese.

By the mid-1990s, there were over 40,000 private businesses in the TAR, mostly Chinese-owned retail shops and restaurants. The region was opened to foreign investment in the 1980s, and companies from China's highly industrialized east coast opened operations in Tibet. Others came from Hong Kong, Taiwan, Malaysia, and the United States.

The Chinese have replaced primitive methods of crop transportation (left) with new tractors (right) on some state farms.

AGRICULTURE

About 2 percent of historical Tibet's land area is used for agriculture. About 85 percent of the farmland is in Kham province. In Ü-Tsang, which makes up most of the Tibet Autonomous Region, temperatures are colder and elevations are higher than in Kham. Crops grow on only about 0.3 percent of Ü-Tsang's land. Here, the best farming regions are the Lhasa and Yarlung Tsangpo river valleys.

Grains account for about 80 percent of the TAR's farm product value. Highland barley—a hardy variety that withstands high altitude and cold weather—is the major crop. Other important crops are winter wheat, rapeseed, corn, rice, millet, buckwheat, potatoes, peas, cabbage, sugar beets, and turnips.

Tibet's abundant sunshine sometimes contributes to high yields and enormous produce. Ü-Tsang has the world's highest wheat yield per acre. It is not unusual for a Tibetan farmer to dig up a 5-pound (2.3-kilogram) potato.

Larger farms use mechanized farm equipment such as plows,

After years of bad management, the Chinese now leave nomads alone to manage their herds on such grazing lands as these in western Tibet.

tractors, and harvesters. However, many farmers still use yak-drawn wooden plows.

After 1959, some farmland became state farms, where workers received a salary but no farm products. Other land was divided into communes, or collective farms. In the 1980s, communal farming was abandoned, and families and farming teams became the basic units of farm production.

The vast plains of the Tibetan Plateau provide pasture for yaks, sheep, goats, and cattle. Horses, mules, donkeys, and ponies graze there, too. The TAR has over 32 million acres (13 million hectares) of pastureland, with about 21 million livestock animals grazing on it. In Amdo province, about 96 percent of the land is pasture.

In the 1960s, the Chinese made drastic changes in livestock management. They confiscated the nomads' herds and organized herders into communes. Yaks, sheep, and goats were redistributed, with each man, woman, and child getting an equal number of animals. On the communes, herders had to fence the pastures, sow grass seed, and build irrigation canals. The results were many depleted pastures and dead animals.

Nomads are now allowed to manage their herds as they used to, although under Chinese supervision. Occasionally an official orders animals to be slaughtered to prevent overgrazing. However, the herders insist that they know what they are doing, as their methods have worked for centuries.

Tibet's pasturelands are getting smaller and are degrading. Many winter pastures at lower elevations are being converted to cropland. This forces the herds to graze on land that would previously have been left alone to renew its growth.

RESOURCES

Traditionally, Tibetans have not developed mining because of ancient religious beliefs. To them, digging into the land disturbs spirits that live there. The Chinese saw mining as a way to derive income from the Tibetan Plateau. Their mining surveys revealed a wealth of deposits. Serious mining began in the 1960s as road-building opened up hard-to-reach areas.

Tibet holds a major share of the world's reserves of lithium, borax, iron ore, uranium, and chromite. Amdo province has the world's largest known lithium deposit, containing half of all the lithium in the world. Iron ore in Tibet's traditional regions constitutes about 2.3 percent of the world's iron reserves. Other valuable deposits include gold, silver, lead, zinc, tin, mercury, coal, salt, arsenic, sulfur, mica, radium, plutonium, and jade.

Mining is the largest sector of industry in Ü-Tsang and Amdo. Mines operate in more than 100 locations in those regions. In the early 1980s, a chromite mine in Lhoka district accounted for half the value of all of the TAR's annual industrial production.

Hot-spring geysers on the Chang Thang in western Tibet have potential for being utilized for electricity.

Most businesses and newer homes in Lhasa receive electricity. Electric power lines also reach some of the smaller towns, especially those near hydroelectric plants. In the west, electrical service is scanty, and most rural areas have none. Tibetans use electricity mainly for lighting, although yak-butter lamps still light most homes.

Tibet's rivers are a great energy source because of their steep drops in elevation. According to water resource experts, Tibet's potential for hydroelectric power is the highest in the world. A number of hydroelectric power plants have been built in Tibet. One large-capacity plant was built at Yamdrok Tso, although it is not operating properly. Another is planned for the "great bend" of the Yarlung Tsangpo River, near the southeastern border.

Geothermal energy is another potential energy source. Tibet has many hot-water springs, whose heat comes from deep in the earth. High winds on the plateau are yet another potential source of energy.

Tibet has the world's second-highest potential for solar energy, after Africa's Sahara Desert. Because of Tibet's high altitude, the sun's radiation is very intense. Some solar energy is used in Lhasa, which gets an average of 3,000 hours of sunshine a year.

Tibet's forests are among its most valuable resources. Conifers—pine, spruce, and fir—are the most important timber species. Other valuable trees are poplar, willow, and cypress.

The thickest forests are in the eastern river valleys of Tibet's traditional Kham province. Political borders run through this region, dividing it among the TAR and China's Yunnan and Sichuan provinces. In the TAR, timber is also harvested in the south-central and southeastern Yarlung Tsangpo River Valley.

Since 1950, the harvesting of timber has drastically reduced Tibet's forestlands. Chinese road-building projects enabled forestry crews to reach areas of dense growth. Then convoys of trucks left Tibet laden with timber. A visitor in 1991 reported watching sixty truckloads of timber leaving one site every hour.

Forests covered about 85,640 square miles (221,800 square kilometers) of historical Tibet in 1985. This is about 5 percent of its total land area, down from 9 percent in 1950. China's timber harvest in Tibetan regions from 1950 to 1985 is estimated at more than $54 billion.

TRANSPORTATION

Before 1950, yaks, ponies, and donkeys were Tibetans' main form of transportation. The thirteenth Dalai Lama owned three automobiles, but the country's roads were not suitable for motor vehicles. Now Chinese-built roads reach many areas of Tibet.

There are two roads by which international travelers may enter

Left: Bicycles are a common form of transportation in cities, especially Lhasa. Right: Mountain roads, such as this one into Nepal, are frequently made impassable by landslides.

and leave the TAR. One is the Nepal-Tibet Highway, crossing the Himalayas at Tibet's southern border with Nepal. The trip between Kathmandu and Lhasa takes several days. The other is the Qinghai-Tibet Highway, running between Lhasa and Golmud (Qinghai province). This trip can take two days or more.

Other major roads connect cities within the TAR and continue beyond the border. Some roads crossing the border are mainly military transport routes for convoys of army trucks. Minor roads thread along the base of the Himalayas and through some areas of the plateau. The roads can be rocky and muddy, and roads on the mountainsides can be precarious.

Within Lhasa, minibuses and rickshaws provide public transportation. Bicycles and even mountain bikes can be rented by the hour or the day. Travelers can take public buses, minibuses, or all-terrain vehicles to a number of sites outside of Lhasa. In Shigatse, tractor drivers give rides for a small fee.

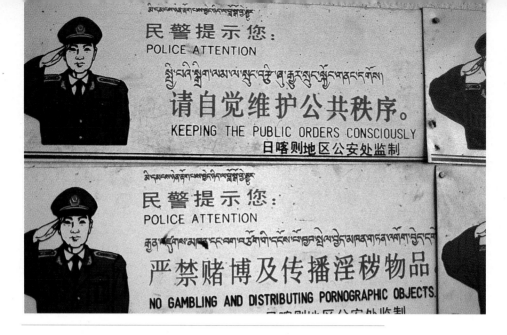

Government warnings in a restaurant are communicated in Chinese, Tibetan, and English.

Lhasa's Gonggar Airport is about 50 miles (80 kilometers) south of Lhasa, a two-hour bus ride from the city. Flights connect only with Kathmandu (Nepal) and Chengdu (Sichuan province). Weather and political factors can affect the flight schedules.

There are no railroads in the Tibet Autonomous Region. On the eastern edge of Amdo province, rail lines connect the towns of Golmud and Xining, continuing on to Lanzhou.

COMMUNICATIONS

The British installed Tibet's first telegraph line in 1904, between Gyantse and Kalimpong. Another line went into service in the 1920s, connecting Gyantse and Lhasa. After 1950, the Chinese built telecommunications stations to serve their mining, power, construction, and military sites.

China has been improving its telephone networks in recent years. According to Chinese authorities, a yak herder on the

Tibetan Plateau can now dial direct to anywhere in the world from his cellular phone. In theory, he probably could. However, this does not give an accurate picture of Tibet's communications systems. Home telephones for Tibetans are rare. Telephone service is available in the Lhasa area but absent in most other places.

Tibet's one daily newspaper, the *Tibet Daily*, is published in Lhasa. It is in Chinese, with a Tibetan-language edition. The *China Daily* is China's English-language newspaper meant for foreigners. The *People's Daily* is the official Communist Party newspaper. No non-Chinese newspapers or magazines are sold in Tibet.

Tibet's government-in-exile publishes information on Tibet that China does not make available. One news magazine is the bimonthly *Tibetan Bulletin*, published in Dharamsala, India. The independent *Tibetan Review* is published in New Delhi, India.

Most radio and television broadcasts are in Chinese. Radio Lhasa began broadcasting in the 1950s. In 1991 Voice of America (VOA) began a daily fifteen-minute Tibetan-language program. In the first broadcast, Tibetans heard the Dalai Lama's voice addressing them for the first time since he went into exile in 1959. Today, VOA broadcasts two one-hour Tibetan programs every day.

Tibet TV in Lhasa broadcast its first show, a color presentation of a Chinese video, in 1979. It is believed that there was only one color television in Tibet at the time. Now there are several thousand. Tibet TV receives programs through a satellite receiver completed in 1985. A second station offers some programming in the Tibetan language.

Major cities have post offices, and mail can be sent and received from Lhasa hotels. Most Tibetans do not ordinarily use postal services, but resident Chinese people use the mail.

Potala Palace on Lhasa's Red Hill
(above) is visible from everywhere
in the city. Even though the Dalai
Lama is no longer in residence,
pilgrims readily explore the palace
(right). The oldest part of Lhasa
surrounds the Jokhang Temple,
where this mother (below)
is praying.

Chapter 11

MONASTERIES, TEMPLES, AND TREASURES

LHASA

Lhasa means "Place of the Gods." At an elevation of 11,830 feet (3,606 meters), it is one of the highest cities in the world. Traditionally, a pilgrim visited Lhasa making three circuits. The Lingkhor was an outer circuit of the city, measuring about 5 miles (8 kilometers). The Barkhor, or inner circuit, circled the Jokhang Temple. It is still much in use today. The third circuit took place inside the temple itself.

Jokhang Temple is in the middle of Lhasa's eastern, or Tibetan, section. It is the holiest place in Lhasa and the spiritual center of all Tibet. Songtsen Gampo built it in the seventh century to house the statues brought by his two Buddhist wives.

Worshipers crowd the front courtyard. Guarding the entrance are four great stone figures, the Lords of the Four Directions. Inside is a maze of rooms and chapels, all lit by the flames of hundreds of flickering yak-butter candles. Imposing statues, beautiful murals, and intricately woven thangkas are everywhere. In the main chapel is the oldest and most honored Buddha statue in Tibet. Called Jowo Sakyamuni, this jewel-encrusted statue was brought to Tibet by Songtsen Gampo's Chinese wife.

Left: A nomad who has made the pilgrimage to Jokhang walks through the Barkhor.
Above: A Chinese guard keeps crowds away from Norbulingka Palace, the Dalai Lama's summer palace.

Encircling the Jokhang is the Barkhor, both a pilgrimage circuit and a teeming marketplace. At the market stalls, people can bargain for jewelry, butter, yak meat, prayer wheels, and even dental services. There are colorfully dressed tribesmen and people walking sheep and dogs, as well as tourists and police.

On the west side of Lhasa, on Red Hill, is the thirteen-story Potala Palace. The name means "high heavenly realm." Its glistening rooftops of gilded copper can be seen from miles away. Golden dragons perch on the roof as protectors. The red-and-white painted stone walls slope slightly inward. In some places the walls are 16 feet (5 meters) thick. Songtsen Gampo began the Potala in the seventh century A.D. as both a palace and a fortress. More construction was done from 1645 to 1694.

Within the Potala's 1,200 rooms are priceless art treasures of gold, silver, and precious stones and libraries of Buddhist manuscripts. It is said to contain 10,000 altars and 200,000 statues.

The Chinese takeover of Tibet has brought influences to Lhasa that were previously unknown to the devout Buddhist culture.

The gilded tombs of eight past Dalai Lamas are housed there, too. The thirteenth Dalai Lama's remains rest in a stupa, 46 feet (14 meters) high. The Potala was the Dalai Lama's winter home, and his apartments are on the top floor.

A smaller palace, Norbulingka ("Jewel Park"), served as the Dalai Lama's summer residence. The graceful yellow building, set in a park, is now a museum.

Lhasa's west side is the Chinese section of town. Near the Potala is a new theater for cultural events. Farther west, near Norbulingka, are modern hotels for foreign visitors.

Just west of Lhasa is Drepung Monastery, its fifteenth-century stone buildings clinging to the mountainside. A great center of the Gelukpa sect, Drepung was once the largest monastery in the world. It housed 10,000 monks and owned vast estates and pasturelands. Today, only about three hundred to four hundred monks live there and work the orchards and grounds.

Drepung is a complex of courtyards, temples, and white-washed stone buildings, with narrow alleyways for streets. The

Most monasteries were destroyed by the Chinese, but parts of Drepung (left), west of Lhasa, and Sera (right), on a hill in northern Lhasa, remain.

principal building is the main assembly hall, with a three-story statue of Maitreya, the future Buddha. When Dalai Lamas came to visit, they stayed in Drepung's Ganden Palace.

Nechung Monastery is a short walk from Drepung. It was the seat of the Nechung Oracle, the state oracle of Tibet, until 1959, when he escaped to India. The oracle spoke for Tibet's protective deity and was consulted on important state matters.

Sera Monastery is built into the side of a hill on the north edge of Lhasa. This Gelukpa monastery was once home to 5,000 monks and now has about 300. Sera's three colleges for Buddhist instruction house innumerable statues, some of them centuries old. In one of its chapels is a two-story Maitreya statue. Monks at Sera hold lively religious debates in the courtyard every afternoon.

CENTRAL TIBET

Nam Tso, northwest of Lhasa, is the second-largest saltwater lake in China. A pilgrim takes about eighteen days to circle it on foot. Along the shore is a bird sanctuary, where thousands of

Yamdrok Tso is a large lake south of Lhasa.

geese and other waterbirds make their nests and raise their young.

West of Lhasa is Tsurphu Monastery. Since the 1100s, it has been the seat of the Karma Kagyud order of monks, called "Black Hats." The name comes from when Kublai Khan presented a black hat to the Karmapa lama in 1256. A boy believed to be the seventeenth reincarnated Karmapa lama now resides at Tsurphu, giving daily blessings to visitors.

East of Lhasa, overlooking the Kyichu Valley, are the remains of Ganden Monastery. This was the first Gelukpa monastery, founded by Tsong Khapa in 1409. Before it was destroyed, Ganden encompassed fifty buildings and housed 7,000 monks. Only a few of the buildings are still intact.

Southeast of Lhasa is the historic Yarlung Valley. The area's capital is Tsetang, which rests at the base of Mount Gongbori. In a cave in this mountain, Tibetans' legendary monkey and ogress became parents of the Tibetan people.

Early Yarlung kings ruled from Yumbu Lakang castle, south of Tsetang. The white-stone castle, perched high on a hill overlooking the valley, was the oldest known building in Tibet. It was

Samye Monastery, Tibet's oldest monastery, lies in a fertile valley (left), made vivid green by summer rains. Colorful cloth hangings are draped in its central building (right).

destroyed in the Cultural Revolution and later rebuilt and redecorated. Some of its original, seventh-century base remains. Inside, murals show scenes from the life of the first king, Nyatri Tsenpo.

Twenty miles (32 kilometers) south of Tsetang, just beyond the town of Chonggye, is the Valley of the Kings. Here, on a desolate plateau, are the burial mounds of eight early Tibetan kings. The largest mound is seventh-century king Songtsen Gampo's tomb, with a temple on top. Inside the temple are statues of the king, his Chinese and Nepalese wives, and his minister, Sambhota, who devised the Tibetan writing system. This tomb has never been opened, but annals tell of a subterranean burial chamber filled with fabulous treasures.

Not much is left of Trandruk Temple, a former monastery just south of Tsetang. However, one of its chapels contains a magnificent thangka showing Chenresi resting. Embroidered into the cloth, it is said, are thirty thousand pearls.

West of Tsetang, on the north side of the Yarlung Tsangpo

River, is Samye Monastery. To get there from Tsetang, travelers must cross the river in a ferry boat, then take a long, rough wagon ride to the monastery. Samye was Tibet's first Buddhist monastery, founded in 779 by King Trisong Detsen and two scholar-saints, Padmasambhava and Santarakshita. Samye's temples and chapels were built in two concentric circles, representing the Buddhist concept of the universe.

TSANG

Shigatse, the old capital of Tsang province, is about 225 miles (362 kilometers) southwest of Lhasa. From Lhasa, it is a day-long trip over treacherous mountain roads, past Yamdrok Tso. There, at the base of Dromari Mountain, are the multi-level, salmon-colored chapels and chanting halls of Tashilhunpo Monastery.

Founded by the first Dalai Lama in 1447, Tashilhunpo is the official seat of the Panchen Lama. The statue of Maitreya in the Great Buddha Hall is Tibet's largest Buddha statue. Standing 87 feet (27 meters) high, it is made of more

A monk plays with his cat at the entrance to a temple in Tashilhunpo Monastery in Shigatse.

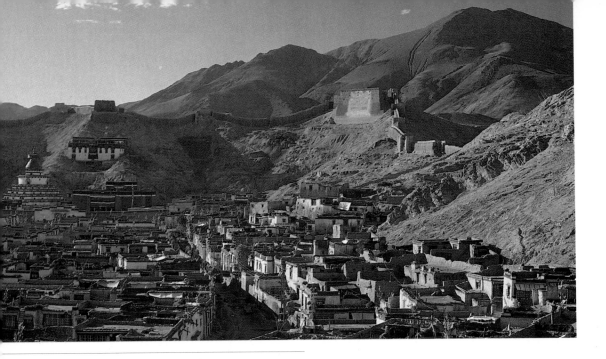

Gyantse is Tibet's fourth largest city.

than 600 pounds (272 kilograms) of gold.

After Lhasa and Shigatse, Tibet's most important city was Gyantse. Since medieval times, it was a center for the wool trade. Caravans lumbered in from the northern plateau laden with yak and sheep wool, which was then exported to China and Nepal. The Gyantse County Rug Factory continues a centuries-old rug-making tradition. Wool is carded, spun, and dyed here, then woven into the bold designs typical of the Tsang region.

In the Palkhor Chöde monastery complex is the Kumbum, the largest stupa in Tibet. A Gyantse prince had it built in 1427, using craftsmen from Nepal. Four tiers of chapels form its massive base. All-seeing eyes look out from four sides of its tall shaft, which is topped by a golden tower. Inside the chapels are elaborate murals and statues.

About 80 miles (128 kilometers) west of Shigatse is Sakya Monastery, one of the most important in Tibet's history. This was

Fields of flowers grow in the fertile Sakya Valley.

the birthplace of the Sakyapa sect and the seat of the Sakya lama, who ruled Tibet under the Mongols. Like a Mongol-style fortress, it is surrounded by high walls with watchtowers at the corners. Inside are several buildings, some from the thirteenth century and others newly built. A towering prayer pole stands in the courtyard before the main hall. Mongol artists painted the murals of the Four Heavenly Kings in the main hall's entryway. Statues in the hall contain the remains of past Sakya lamas. The monastery walls, and also the buildings in Sakya village, are painted a maroon color instead of white.

West of Sakya is Lhatse. The road to Nepal, or Friendship Highway, branches off to the southwest of Lhatse. Along this road, about 10 miles (16 kilometers) north of Nyalam, is Milarepa's Cave. Milarepa was a saintly poet who spent many years here as a hermit, and monks still tend the cave.

Continuing on toward the border town of Dram (Zhangmu to

Chiu Monastery, by Lake Manasarovar, commands a view of holy Mt. Kailas in the Ngari region.

the Chinese), one travels a steep, treacherous road of hairpin curves. Traders used to call this mountain pass the Gate of Hell. The scenery is breathtaking, though, with towering cliffs, dense pine forest, cascading waterfalls, and mossy riverbeds.

NGARI

Tibet's westernmost province is Ngari. Most people who venture out to the far west are going to Mt. Kailas and Lake Manasarovar. Outside of Lhasa, these are Tibet's holiest pilgrimage sites. In this region, too, are the sources of four great rivers: the Brahmaputra (Yarlung Tsangpo), Sutlej, Indus, and Ganges.

Leaving Lhatse, travelers can take a northern route or a southern route to Mt. Kailas. It takes about a week to get there by the northern route. The southern route offers beautiful Himalayan scenery and takes about four days. This way leads to Purang, where a secondary road heads north to Lake Manasarovar.

One of a pair of lakes, Manasarovar is the highest freshwater lake in the world. Its clear waters reflect the snowy peak of Mt. Kailas, farther north. Hindu pilgrims bathe in the lake, while

Buddhists circle around it.

Mt. Kailas, called the Snow Jewel, is a sacred mountain in Hindu, Buddhist, Bön, and Jain religions. All Tibetan Buddhists hope to make at least one pilgrimage to Mt. Kailas before they die. It is said that circling Mt. Kailas once removes the sins of a lifetime, and 108 circuits leads straight to nirvana.

West of Mt. Kailas is Guge, one of medieval Tibet's great western kingdoms. Guge's once-fertile terrain is slowly turning to desert. Thöling and Tsaparang were Guge's capital cities and centers of Buddhist learning. Their monastery complexes, once impressive, are now mostly in ruins. Exotic murals in a chapel at Tsaparang are rare examples of the early art of Kashmir. Guge's capital is Shiquanhe, on the highway leading north to the Xinjiang Autonomous Region.

KHAM

Chamdo, the TAR's third-largest city, was the capital of Kham province. Formerly, one-quarter of Chamdo's people were monks. Now many residents of Chamdo are Chinese people working in various industries. East of Chamdo, the road crosses the Mekong and Yangtze rivers and the Tibet Autonomous Region's border with Sichuan province.

Tibetans seen in this region are nomadic Khampa tribespeople. Famous as warriors, the Khampas fought off Chinese attacks in the early decades of the 1900s. Khampa horsemen also served as the Dalai Lama's bodyguards, escorting him safely out of Tibet.

Just inside the Sichuan border is the town of Derge. Derge's monastery has been a great printing center since the 1700s.

Hundreds of thousands of printing woodblocks are stacked high against the walls. Monks print volumes of scriptures by hand, spreading ink across the raised letters, then smoothing paper across the inked surface. The books are so holy that pilgrims even bow before puddles of ink. Buddhists from all over Asia come to see the monastery's vast collection of scriptures.

AMDO

Most of Amdo province became China's Qinghai province in the first half of the twentieth century. From Lhasa, the long trip into Qinghai crosses the border at a snowy pass through the Tanggula Mountains. It continues on to Golmud in central Qinghai. On the stark and empty landscape along the way, one may see a herd of gazelles or an occasional sheepherder. From Golmud, a road to the east leads to Xining, Qinghai's capital.

Nearby Kumbum Monastery, on Tsong Khapa's birth site, was one of the great centers of the Gelukpa sect. The present Dalai Lama was also born in the area. Once a vital spiritual center, Kumbum now operates on a smaller scale. Eight great stupas stand at the entrance, and several temples can be visited. Kumbum's monks create exquisite butter sculptures for religious festivals.

West of Xining is Kokonor (Qinghai Lake in Chinese), China's largest saltwater lake. Its level rises with the spring thaws. Kokonor is dotted with many sandy islands. Bird Island, on its western edge, swarms with thousands of nesting birds in the spring. Nomads graze their sheep on the lush, grassy steppes around Kokonor—Mongols on the north side and Tibetans on the south. No one seems to mind sharing.

People, such as this Golok family of the Amdo region, are what the Tibetan struggle is all about. Tibetans are losing their identity through Chinese immigration and control.

THE FUTURE

Realistically, few people truly expect that Tibetans will regain full religious freedom or recapture their former way of life. Many doubt that the Dalai Lama will be able to conduct significant negotiations with China's leaders.

Tibet is too valuable for China to let it go. From Tibet, China has a strong strategic position against the rest of Asia. China has also come to rely on Tibet's resources—its timber, minerals, and energy supplies. Even Tibet's emptiness is an asset. The unspoiled frontiers are ideal sites for foreign investment and for waste dumping. Both are good sources of income for China.

Meanwhile, international organizations are making sure the outside world is aware of Tibet's predicament. Constant publicity lets China know that the world is watching. With enough international pressure, the surviving Tibetans may one day enjoy basic human rights. Perhaps, as a Chinese dissident leader said, Tibet's problems will not end until democracy comes to China.

The Dalai Lama remains optimistic. "Oppression cannot last. It is contrary to human nature," he insists. "The dominant trait in human nature is compassion."

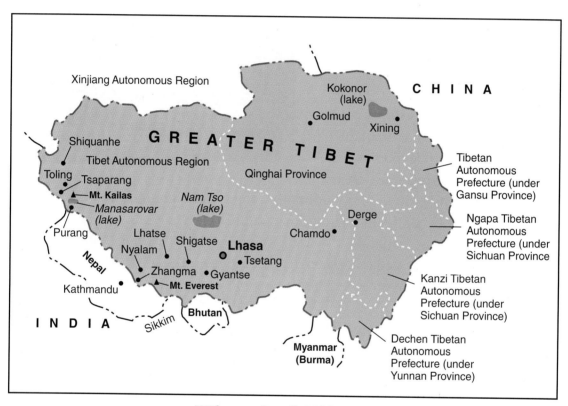

Historical Tibet
with Today's Political Boundaries

MINI-FACTS AT A GLANCE

GENERAL INFORMATION

Official Name: The historically independent Tibet is presently under Chinese occupation. It has been divided into the Tibet Autonomous Region (TAR, called Xizang in Chinese) and other areas presently under China's Qinghai, Yunnan, Gansu, and Sichuan provinces.

Capital: Lhasa.

Government: In 1959 the Dalai Lama established a government-in-exile as a continuation of Tibet's pre-1959 government. It consists of the Kashag (the executive branch), an elected Assembly of Tibetan People's Deputies, a Supreme Justice Commission, and eight administrative departments. There are offices representing the Dalai Lama's government in almost every part of the world.

According to the government-in-exile's proposed constitution of 1963, Tibet will have executive, legislative, and judicial branches of government. It is hoped that Tibet will eventually have its own elected government, and then the government-in-exile will cease to exist.

China has divided the TAR into seven prefectures and one regional municipality, Lhasa.

Religion: Buddhism is the predominant religion among Tibetans. Some also practice the ancient Bön religion, worshiping spirits in nature. Small numbers of Hindus, Muslims, and Christians live in Tibet. Religion is the force behind Tibetan culture, arts, and daily life. Banned and destroyed after the 1959 Chinese takeover, some of the monasteries are slowly reopening. Chenresi (Indian: Avalokiteshvara), or the bodhisattva of compassion, is the main deity. Tibet's patron goddess is Dolma (Indian: Tara).

Ethnic Composition: Tibetan and Chinese people are the major ethnic groups in the TAR. China claims that Tibetans make up 96 percent of the TAR, while outside agencies estimate that there may be as few as 60 percent. Several small ethnic minorities also live in the TAR.

Language: The Mandarin dialect of Chinese is the official language, although Tibetan is most widely spoken. It belongs to the Tibeto-Burman language group.

National Calendar: The Tibetan calendar breaks time into sixty-year cycles with each year matched to one of five elements—iron, water, wood, earth, or fire. The months of the Tibetan year are about six weeks later than months in the

Gregorian calendar. The year 1997 on the Gregorian (Western) calendar is Tibetan year 2124.

Money: Chinese currency is in use. In May 1996, 8.4 Chinese yuan were equal to $1 US.

Population: 1990 census of the TAR, 2,196,010; 1992 estimate, 2,260,000; 5 persons per sq. mi. (2 persons per sq km). There are also some 81,000 to 1.4 million Chinese people living in the TAR. The population of historical Tibet is estimated at 6 million.

Cities:

> Lhasa . . . . 330,000 (1990 census)
> Shigatse . . . . 40,000 (1980 estimate)
> (Figures on smaller cities not available)

GEOGRAPHY

Border: To the south of the TAR are India, Bhutan, Myanmar (Burma), and Nepal. Almost one-half of the TAR's border is with China—Xinjiang Autonomous Region is to the northwest, Qinghai province is to the northeast, Sichuan province is to the east, and Yunnan province is to the southeast.

Land: One of the most isolated places in the world, Tibet is a mountainous and rugged region. Situated on a high plateau, it is enclosed by even higher mountains and is sometimes called the Roof of the World. Average elevation is about 15,000 ft. (4,600 m). Tibet's northern plain region, Chang Thang, is a high and barren desolate plain of rocks with few valleys, lakes, and grassy plains. The TAR's southern and eastern border regions make up the Outer Plateau, which has several river valleys; here is the region's best agricultural land.

Mountains: The Himalayas form most of the southern border and extend from east to west. Several tall peaks, including Mt. Everest, the world's tallest mountain, are at the border with Nepal. Other noteworthy peaks are Lhotse I, Makalu I, Lhotse II, and Cho Oyu. The Karakoram Range makes Tibet's northwestern border, and the Kunlun Mountains make its northern boundary. The permanent snowline is between 16,000 and 20,000 feet (4,878 and 6,096 m). Mt. Kailas is sacred to both Buddhists and Hindus and is one of Tibet's holiest site.

Highest Point: Mt. Everest, 29,028 ft. (8,848 m); called *Chomolungma* ("Goddess Mother Goddess of the World") in Tibetan.

Rivers: The Yarlung Tsangpo (Indian: Brahmaputra) is Tibet's longest river, flowing from west to east for about 1,278 mi. (2,057 km); it turns south into India and eventually empties into the Bay of Bengal. Headwaters of the Ganges, Indus, Sutlej, and Yarlung Tsangpo are in the Kailas Range.

Lakes: There are more than 1,500 lakes scattered through historical Tibet; most of them are saltwater lakes. Lake Kokonor is the largest saltwater lake in China and Nam Tso is the second-largest. Yamdrok Tso is Tibet's largest freshwater lake. Mapham Tso (Manasarovar Lake) is one of Buddhism's holiest sites and is the highest freshwater lake in the world. Salt deposits in the numerous dry lake beds provide the Tibetans with salt.

Forests: Forests, covering about 5 percent of historical Tibet's land area, are among Tibet's most valuable resources. Pine, spruce, fir, poplar, willow, and cypress are the most important timber species. Almost no tree or woody plant grows at elevations higher than 16,000 ft.(4,877 m); only algae, mosses, and lichens thrive at that altitude. Forests of oak, elm, ash, juniper, willows, maple, and birch trees are in the TAR's south and east. Evergreen species include pine, spruce, fir, and hemlock. In the warmer southern region, banana and tea plants are grown. More than a thousand types of medicinal herbs and 300 species of rhododendron grow in Tibet. Historical Tibet suffers from severe deforestation—more than 40 percent of its pre-1950 forests have been cut.

Wildlife: In the Tibetan forests live black and brown bears, red pandas, musk deer, barking deer, tigers, snow leopards, lynxes, wild yaks, monkeys, and squirrels. The blue sheep, ibex, and wild goat roam the high rocky mountainsides. Tibet has more than 500 species of birds including snow finches, doves, robins, snow grouse, vultures, bar-headed geese, brown-head gulls, and swans. More than thirty animal species are classified as endangered.

Climate: Tibet's climate is marked with low humidity and extreme temperatures. December, January, and February are the coldest months when temperatures can plunge to 0° F. (–40° C). May and June are the mildest months, and average July temperatures are around 58° F. (14° C). Windstorms, blizzards, and snowstorms are common. Much of the snow remains on the ground all year round in the mountain areas. Northern and western Tibet receive the least rainfall. Central Tibet receives about 15 to 20 in. (38 to 50 cm) of precipitation in the form of snow or rain. Half of Tibet's rainfall occurs in the months of July and August, although the country does not receive true monsoon storms.

Greatest Distance: North to South: 620 mi. (992 km)
East to West: 2,030 mi. (3,248 km).
Area: 471,700 sq. mi. (1,221,700 sq km).

ECONOMY AND INDUSTRY

Agriculture: Historically, agriculture and livestock have been Tibet's chief economic activities. Grains (barley, winter wheat, rapeseed, corn, rice, millet) account for about 80 percent of Tibet's farm product value; other crops are potatoes, peas, cabbage, sugar beets, and turnips. Agriculture provides livelihood to some 900,000 Tibetans. Larger farms use some mechanized farm equipment and smaller farms use yak-driven wooden plows. Livestock includes yaks, horses, sheep, goats, cattle, mules, donkeys, and ponies. Yaks are all-purpose beasts used to transport trade goods, household belongings, and tents, and are also used on farms. Yaks provide milk, meat, hides, and dung (used as fuel). The coarse outer hair is made into ropes and slingshots, while the softer hair is pounded into felt for tents and boots.

Mining: Mining is the largest sector of the TAR's industry. Chinese mining surveys have revealed a wealth of mineral deposits in Tibet including lithium, borax, iron ore, uranium, gold, silver, lead, zinc, tin, mercury, coal, salt, arsenic, sulfur, mica, radium, plutonium, jade, and chromite. The world's largest known lithium deposits are in Amdo province.

Manufacturing: China operates five nuclear bases and its largest ICBM (intercontinental ballistic missile) site in Tibet. In the 1960s, China built a major nuclear weapons research facility in Amdo (Qinghai) near Lake Kokonor. China has developed mining and manufacturing industries such as ironwork, woodwork, and a tannery in the TAR. Presently, there are some 200 small and medium-sized factories manufacturing small machinery, textiles, carpets, chemicals, and books. Handicrafts include carpets, clothing, and wood and metal crafts.

Transportation: Before China's invasion in 1951, yaks, ponies, and donkeys were commonly used for transportation. The few roads were not suitable for motor vehicles. The Nepal-Tibet Highway crosses the Himalayas at Tibet's southern border, and the Qinghai-Tibet Highway runs between Lhasa and Golmud (Qinghai province). Mudslides often hamper travel in mountainous areas. Public transportation in cities is provided by minibuses and rickshaws. The Gonggar International Airport is 50 mi. (80 km) from Lhasa. There are no railroads in the TAR, but China has built new roads. In the early 1990s, there were 13,651 mi. (21,842 km) of roads in the TAR, of which some 30 percent were paved.

Communications: The TAR's only daily newspaper, the *Tibet Daily,* is published in Lhasa in Chinese and Tibetan. Tibet's government-in-exile publishes information on Tibet from Dharamsala, India. Most radio and television broadcasts are in Chinese.

Trade: Before the Chinese takeover, Tibet used to export wool, animal skins and products, medicinal herbs, borax, mica, and salt to India, Nepal, Bhutan, and China, and import tea, silk, porcelain, textiles, sugar, rice, fuels, rice, and dried fruits from the neighboring countries.

EVERYDAY LIFE

Health: Tibetans in general are healthy people. In the early 1990s, Tibetan life expectancy varied between 40 and 61 years; the infant-mortality rate is high. Accessibility to safe drinking water is low, and water near nuclear facilities is dangerous. Influenza, pneumonia, and tuberculosis are common illnesses. Hospitals and clinics are generally established in cities with Chinese population. Lhasa's Tibetan Medical Center provides traditional medical treatment. More than one thousand medicinal herbs are used in preparing Tibetan medicines and remedies. The Department of Health of the government-in-exile manages dozens of hospitals, clinics, and health-care centers for refugees.

Education: The Chinese abolished religious schooling in Tibet and established a secular school system. The schooling consists of primary and secondary schools, with few middle schools. Cities with a Chinese population have school facilities. Tibet University is in Lhasa. In the early 1990s, the literacy rate was only about 22 percent. Historically, Buddhist monasteries also served as schools, but under Chinese rule, children cannot study there. The Department of Education of the government-in-exile operates some 90 primary, middle, and secondary schools for refugees. In the late 1980s, there were some 14 technical schools and three institutions of higher learning.

Holidays: Tibetans celebrate festivals throughout the year. Losar is the New Year festival, when monks perform a spectacular dance-drama to drive out the evils of the old year and bring in good luck for the new year. Great Prayer Festival (Mönlam) begins three days after New Year. Buddha's Anniversary festival is celebrated in May and the Incense Festival is in June. Chökor Düchen honors Buddha's first sermon. The Chinese have introduced holidays such as Labor Day (May 1) and the anniversary of the founding of the Tibet Autonomous Region (September 1).

Culture: Historically, Tibet was a crossroads for cultural exchange, and it has developed a unique culture of its own. Tibetan art often depicts a mandala, a design with a central deity encircled by other beings and symbols. Monks painstakingly create mandalas as a spiritual exercise by using grains of colored sand. *Gesar*, the longest Tibetan epic, is known to have two to three million verses. Other major works of literature are the 108-volume *Kangyur*, and 227-volume *Tengyur*. The *Tibetan Book of the Dead (Bardo Thodol)* is a book of instruction about death and dying. An estimated 60 percent of Tibetan literature has been systematically destroyed by the Chinese. The Tibetan Medical and Astro. Institute, the Library of Tibetan Works and Archives, and the Tibetan Children's Village are at Dharamsala, India.

Society: Presently, Tibetan family size is controlled by Chinese law. Families in the rural areas may have three children, but those in towns may have only two. Nomads live in camps of several families each and tend yaks, sheep, and goats. They travel in a caravan from pasture to pasture. Men tend livestock while women tan hides, spin wool, sew clothes, weave blankets, strip and dry yak meat, and make butter, yogurt, and cheese. Nomads trade wool, meat, butter, salt, medicinal herbs, and hides for barley, rice, flour, and tea.

Before the Chinese invasion, monasteries functioned as universities, art museums, charitable foundations, landlords, and money-lending institutions in Tibetan society. Lamas are monks of exceptional wisdom and deep spirituality, and are believed to be the reincarnation of great lamas who lived before them. The Dalai Lama is considered a manifestation of Chenresi, the bodhisattva of compassion.

Customs: Marriages are arranged by parents. Astrologers or monks determine the best time for the marriage ceremony. Buddhists pray while circumambulating, or walking round and round, a holy place. They turn prayer wheels as much as possible, as each rotation of the wheel is considered a recitation of a prayer. Rosary beads are used for prayer and chanting. Tibetans recycle the dead body by feeding it to ravens and vultures. Burial in the ground is very rare, and so are cremations because wood for fire is scarce.

Dress: In cities, Western dress is becoming popular. However, the majority of Tibetans still prefer traditional dress. Women wear black dresses or black shirts, skirts, or pants. They tie a brightly colored wool apron over the dress. Turquoise beads are commonly worn by Tibetan women in their hair. Some women braid their hair in 108 strands, a sacred number for the Buddhist. Women wear earrings, bracelets, headbands, and belts of semiprecious stones. Men wear loose shirts and pants. A sheepskin or woolen *chuba* is worn over the clothes and tied at the middle. High boots are made of yak skin and hide. Buddhist monks wear traditional burgundy-colored one-piece robes.

Housing: Tibetan homes are generally made of brick or stone. They are one or two stories high and have earthen floors. The roof is flat with a wall around the edge. The first floor is used for cooking, eating, socializing, prayers, and storage. The second floor is used for sleeping. Most homes do not have electricity, and indoor plumbing is rare. Nomads live in large tents made of yak-hair felt. Most tents have a wooden churn for making butter and a loom for weaving rugs, blankets, and cloth. Sometimes stone walls are built around tents to stop the bitterly cold winds. Yak dung is the most common fuel and yak-butter lamps illuminate most houses.

Handicrafts and Tourism: Thangkas are Tibet's traditional cloth paintings depicting Buddhist deities or themes in intricate details. Artisans make various religious objects, *gau* (amulets), hand-knotted wool carpets, aprons, yak-hide saddles and shoes, pottery, and wood carvings. Some 30,000 tourists visit Tibet annually, mostly to see Buddhist monasteries.

Food: Yak-butter tea is Tibet's national drink. *Chang,* or barley beer, is a common social drink. *Tsampa* is the staple food made of roasted barley and peas ground together. *Thukpa* is a noodle broth with bits of meat and vegetables. Nomads prepare chewy strips of yak or lamb meat that can be kept without refrigeration for long periods of time. Yogurt, yak curds, and cheese balls are common snack items.

Recreation: Sacred music and dance were once a part of everyday Tibetan life. Himalayan long horns, trumpets, conch shells, oboes, finger cymbals, bells, and drums are essential parts of music. Ritual dance called *cham* is a feature of many Tibetan festivals. The cham dancers wear masks of animals or spirits.

Refugees: After 1959, some 80,000 Tibetans took refuge in India, Bhutan, Nepal, and the former kingdom of Sikkim. Today some 100,000 Tibetan refugees live in 46 settlements on the Indian subcontinent. Tibetan refugees have settled in 33 countries around the world, including Switzerland, the United States, Australia, and France. Some 4 million Tibetans live outside the TAR. Slowly, Tibetan refugees are being assimilated into the host societies. Refugee monks have founded new Drepung, Sera, and Ganden monasteries in southern India.

Social Welfare: Tibetan communities outside Tibet generate money to operate refugee settlements. Other funds come from public and private contributions.

IMPORTANT DATES

779—Tibet's first Buddhist monastery is founded by King Trisong Detsen.

1015—Buddhist monks seal a cave in Dunhuang with a library of twenty thousand documents dating from the fifth to the tenth century.

1042—Atisha, the great Buddhist scholar from India, arrives in Tibet to teach Buddhist scriptures.

1073—The Buddhist order of Sakyapa is founded at Sakya Monastery.

1247—Godan, Genghis Khan's grandson, invites Sakya Pandita to meet him; he makes Sakya Pandita viceroy of Tibet, starting the patron-priest relationship that lasted over a century.

1270—Kublai Khan converts to Buddhism.

1280—Mongols conquer China and establish Yuan Dynasty.

1354—The Kagyupa sect defeats the Sakyapa sect and gains power.

1368—The Chinese overthrow the Mongols in China and establish the Ming dynasty.

1409—Ganden Monastery is founded.

1416—Gelukpa Monastery is founded.

1419—Sera Monastery is founded.

1435—The ruling Kagyupa monks are ousted by Tsang princes.

1445—Tashilhunpo Monastery is founded by Gedun Drup; it is the official seat of the Panchen Lama.

1565—Rule of Tsang princes ends in Tibet.

1578—Sonam Gyatso is given the title of *Dalai Lama* for the first time, a tradition that continues today.

1611—The Tsang king attacks Drepung and Sera monasteries.

1642—Mongol Gushri Khan invades Tibet and conquers Tsang province.

1644—Manchus establish the Qing Dynasty in China.

1706—Mongol prince Lhabzang Khan invades Tibet.

1720—Manchu troops take over Lhasa.

1788—Gurkha warriors invade Tibet from Nepal; with Chinese help, Tibet repels the Gurkha attack; after this incident, Tibet is closed to foreigners.

1841-42—Indian Kingdom of Jammu and Tibet engage in war.

1854-55—Nepal and Tibet engage in a war.

1903—British troops attack Lhasa.

1904—Tibet's first telegraph lines are started.

1906—Trade is opened between Tibet and Great Britain.

1910—Manchus invade Tibet; the Dalai Lama escapes to India (returns in 1913).

1913-14—The Simla Conference is called by the British to arrange an agreement between China and Tibet; British recognize Tibet's independence by agreeing on the Indo-Tibet border.

1947—India gains independence from Britain; British advisers are pulled out from Tibet.

1950—China, under Mao Zedong, launches a full-scale invasion of Tibet.

1951—China presents Tibet a seventeen-point plan that would allow Tibet to keep its religious freedom but give up political freedom; Dalai Lama appeals to the United Nations but gets no support.

1956—Rebellious Khampa tribesmen and monks are brutally crushed by the Chinese; Litang Monastery is destroyed by bombing.

1959—China takes over Tibet completely; in a mass uprising in Lhasa, thousands of Tibetans are killed; the Dalai Lama escapes to India in disguise; many palaces, monasteries, and the Medical College are bombed and destroyed; the International Commission of Jurists condemns the Chinese invasion of Tibet.

1963—The Tibetan government-in-exile drafts a new constitution for Tibet; it combines a Buddhist outlook with modern issues.

1964—The Panchen Lama denounces Chinese policy in Tibet, and he is sentenced to ten years in Chinese prison.

1965—China officially establishes the Tibet Autonomous Region.

1966—China's Cultural Revolution is imposed on Tibet; the Dalai Lama is declared an enemy of the people.

1970—The Tibetan Youth Congress is established by the government-in-exile to train young Tibetans in taking part in their government.

1980—Under international pressure, China sends its own observers to Tibet to study the situation; China opens Tibet's borders for trade and tourism.

1982—Tibetans are evacuated from the Lop Nor region after China conducted nuclear tests.

1984—A Buddhist seminary is opened in Lhasa with 200 students.

1985—Limited religious festivals are allowed; a university is opened in Lhasa.

1986—Tibetans are allowed to celebrate Mönlam for the first time since 1959.

1987—Monks in Lhasa stage a pro-independence demonstration for nine days, several people are killed; the Dalai Lama addresses the U.S. Congress's Human Rights Caucus on the plight of Tibetan people.

1988—The Tibetan language is reinstated as a "major official language" by Chinese government; in his Strasbourg Proposal, the Dalai Lama details a framework for Tibet's future.

1989—The Panchen Lama, free from Chinese jail, criticizes the Chinese once again for their experiment in Tibet; he dies under mysterious conditions a few days later. Lhasa is put under martial law. The Dalai Lama is awarded the Nobel Peace Prize.

1990—The Dalai Lama proposes a compromise with China, but it is rejected; the U.S. Congress passes a law allowing 1,000 immigrant visas to be issued to Tibetan refugees.

1991—The Voice of America (VOA) starts a daily 15-minute Tibetan language broadcast that enables Tibetans to hear the Dalai Lama's voice for the first time since 1959.

1993—The Dalai Lama puts forward another plan of compromise with China, but it is again rejected; major demonstrations are held in Tibet against China; the Dalai Lama receives the Franklin Delano Roosevelt Freedom Medal.

1995—The Dalai Lama names a six-year-old boy from a remote nomad village as the eleventh Panchen Lama—the second most important Buddhist monk in Tibetan Buddhism; this choice is angrily rejected by China; China names its own version of the Panchen Lama; Tibetans stage a hunger strike in New York during the fiftieth anniversary celebration of the United Nations; Phuntsok Nyidron, a nun and freedom fighter in a Tibetan prison, is awarded the Reebok Human Rights Award.

IMPORTANT PEOPLE

Atisha (11th century), a great Indian scholar who came to Tibet to teach Buddhism.

Bhrikuti, a Nepali princess, wife of Songtsen Gampo; helped convert him to Buddhism.

Trisong Detsen (8th century), the Second Religious King; became king in 755; invited great Buddhist scholars from India to teach Buddhism in Tibet.

Songtsen Gampo (608-650), a son of Namri Songtsen, a powerful king whose kingdom covered not only Tibet but parts of Nepal, India, Bhutan, and China; known as the First Religious King, he made Tibet a Buddhist state.

Gampopa (12th century), a Buddhist monk; founded the Karmapa order.

Gedun Drup, the first Dalai Lama, founded Tashilhunpo Monastery; promised before his death that he would reincarnate.

Godan, Genghis Khan's grandson; ruled Tibet in the thirteenth century.

Changchub Gyaltsen (14th century), monk of Kagyupa sect; defeated the Sakyapa sect; he tried to wipe out all traces of Mongols and make the country truly Tibetan; he and his eleven successors ruled Tibet for almost a century.

Ngawang Lobsang Gyatso (1617–1682), also called the Great Fifth; the fifth Dalai Lama and a brilliant scholar, he is honored as the greatest leader in Tibetan history; he made Lhasa Tibet's capital and expanded Potala Palace.

Sonam Gyatso (16th century), the third abbot of Drepung Monastery and a great master of the Gelukpa sect; the third Dalai Lama although the first one to receive title of *Dalai Lama,* ("Ocean of Wisdom").

Tenzin Gyatso (1935-), the fourteenth Dalai Lama, a spiritual leader of all Tibetans; living in exile in India; winner of 1989 Nobel Peace Prize.

Thupten Gyatso (1876–1933), the thirteenth Dalai Lama, considered one of Tibet's greatest reformers; he spent almost two decades trying to modernize Tibet.

Kublai Khan (1215-1294), great-grandson of Genghis Khan; converted to Buddhism; initiated title of Imperial Preceptor (ruler) over Tibet for Phagpa, a Buddhist monk.

Tsong Khapa (1357–1419), established the Gelukpa order ("Virtuous Ones"), also known as the "Yellow Hats."

Langdarma (?- 842), brother of King Ralpachen but a fiercely anti-Buddhist king who demolished monasteries and burned religious books.

Marpa (11th century), Buddhist scholar who founded the Kagyupa sect of Buddhism.

Milarepa (12th century), a Buddhist monk-poet.

Phuntsok Nyidron, a Buddhist nun and a Tibetan freedom fighter; awarded the Reebok Human Rights Award in 1995.

Padmasambhava (8th century), also called *Guru Rinpoche* ("Precious One"); a Buddhist scholar and mystic; established Samye, Tibet's first monastery and university; founded the Nyingmapa ("Ancient Ones") order of Buddhism.

Ralpachen (805-838), a Buddhist king also known as the Third Religious King.

Thonmi Sambhota, a minister of King Songtsen Gampo; he devised a Tibetan alphabet and script based on India's Sanskrit script.

Santarakshita (8th century), Buddhist scholar from India; brought Buddhist teachings to Tibet; cofounder and abbot of Samye Monastery; translated volumes of Buddhist text from Sanskrit to Tibetan.

Namri Songtsen (570-619), the thirty-second king of Tibet, also known as the Commander of 100,000 Warriors.

Nyatri Tsenpo (5th century B.C.), the first Tibetan king.

Wencheng, a Chinese princess who was married to Songtsen Gampo.

Yeshe Ö (11th century), king of Guge who became a monk and brought the scholar Atisha from India.

Compiled by Chandrika Kaul, Ph.D.

INDEX

Page numbers that appear in boldface type indicate illustrations

abbot 59, 74, 76, 81, 82, 153
abortions 34, 100
acupuncture 35
aerial bombs 94
Africa 124
agricultural land 14, 23, 144
agriculture 27, 97, 117, 118, 120, 146
air pollution 34
Alaska 113
algae 23, 145
all-terrain vehicles 125
alphabet 30, 73, 153
alpine wild goat, see ibex
Altan Khan 82
altars 41, 45, 47, 58, **61**, 63, 81, 130
Altyn Tagh mountain range 15
ambans 86, 88
Amdo province 11, 12, 25, 27, 88, 91, 105,
  106, 116, 121, 122, 125, 126, 140, **141**, 144,
  146
Amitabha 61
Amnesty International 113
amulet cases, see gau
ancient texts 34
animals **12**, 19, 20, **21**, **22**, 23, 25, 35, 40,
  45, 46, 47, 49, **57**, 67, 71, 98, 121, 122,
  124, 130, 133, **135**, 140, 145, 146
animism 51
antelopes 20, 22, 35, 98
apprenticeship programs 31
archeologists 71
architecture 65
army 88, 91, 94, 98, 116, 125
art dealers 97
art museums 59, 148
artillery 96, 97
artists 31, 59, **62**, 63, 87, 137, 149
arts 8, 51, 62, 63, 97, 110, 143, 147
ash trees 23, 145
Asian wild ass **20**, 22
Assembly of Tibetan People's Deputies
  109, 111, 112, 143
astrology 42, 64, 148
Atisha 75, 76, 81, 149, 152
Australia 110, 113, 149
automobiles 124
autonomous regions 115, 116
Avalokiteshvara, see Chenresi
Awesome Voice 65, 66
aweto caterpillar 20
azaleas 23

ballistic missiles 94, 116
bamboo forest **25**
banana trees 24, 145
Bangladesh 16
bar-headed geese 20, 145
Bardo Thodol, see *Book of the Dead*

Barkhor 63, 68, 129, **130**
barking deer 19, 145
barley **19**, 37, 47, 58, 59, 98, 146, 148, 149
barley beer 37, 149
barley cakes 47
bartering 118
Bathing Festival 68, 69
Bay of Bengal 16, 144
bears 19, **21**, 35, 145
Beijing 104
bells 65, 149
Bhrikuti 72, 152
Bhutan 8, 12, 28, 29, 52, 72, 96, 110, 112,
  116, 144, 147, 149, 152
bicycles **31**, **119**, **125**
birch trees 23, 145
Bird Island 140
bird sanctuary 132
birds 20, **21**, **22**, 140, 145
biscuits 38
Black Hats 133
black-necked crane **22**
blankets 45, 47, 48, 148, 149
blue sheep 20, 145
boats 48, **49**
bodhisattva 54, **55**, 61
bodhisattva of compassion, see Chenresi
bodily humors 34, 35
bodily sustainers 35
Bön culture 52
Bön lama **52**
Bön priests 74
Bön religion 51, 52, 56, 74, 139, 143
Bönpo 51, 52, 56
Book of the Dead 64, 147
books 30, **59**, 65, 75, 119, 140, 146
boots 48, 146, 148
borax 122, 146, 147
borders 12, **15**, 72, 88, 116, 144, 151
Brahmaputra, see Yarlung Tsangpo River
Brazil **113**
bread **38**
breakfast 47
brick-making **119**
Britain 86, 87, 91, 99, 150
British 86, **87**, 88, 91, 126, 150
British India 87
brown-head gulls 20, 145
Budapest 110
Buddha 52, **53**, 54, 55, 56, 58, 64, 68, 69,
  129, 132, 135, 147
buddhas 63, 68
Buddha's Anniversary Festival 68, 147
Buddhism 8, 17, 51, 52, 53, 54, 55, 56, 58,
  75, 76, **77**, 81, 82, **131**, 143, 145, 150, 152,
  153
Buddhist 10, 17, **52**, **57**, 58, 62, 71, 72, 73,
  75, 93, 102, 107, 111, 129, 132, 135, 139,

140, 144, 147, 148, 149, 151, 152
Buddhist shrine 106
Buddhist texts 6, 7, 30, 39, 54, **64**, 74, 130
burial **58**, 134, 148
burial mounds 71, 134
Burma, see Myanmar
Bush, George 109
business 27, 31, 123
Butter Festival **68**

cabbage 38, 146, 149
calendar 66, 67, 143, 144
Canada 113
Canberra 110
candles 47
caravan 45
carpets **36**, **63**, 119, 146, 149
castle 133
cattle 121, 146
cellular phone 127
Chakna Dorje 54
cham **66**, 149
Chamdo 93, 116, 139
chang, see barley beer
Chang Thang **13**, 16, 17, 23, 27, **34**, **123**,
  144
Chang Thang Wildlife Reserve **22**
Changchub Gyaltsen 77, 78, 152
chanting 8, 65, 135
chapels 129, 132, 135, 136, 139
charms 63
cheese 38, 47, 148, 149
Chengdu 126
Chenresi 54, 58, 61, 71, 134, 143, 148
chieftains 8, 72, 75, 78
children **26**, **31**, **32**, **34**, **36**, 43, **45**, 46, 47,
  92, **104**
China 6, 8, 9, 11, 12, 17, 22, 27, 28, 29, 31,
  33, 42, 54, 60, 71, 72, 73, 75, 76, 77, 78,
  84-88, 91, **92**, 93, 94, 95, 97, 99-104, 108,
  109, 115, 116, 117, 124, 125, 126, 136, 140,
  144, 145, 146, 147, 150, 151, 152
China Daily 127
Chinese 15, 16, 20, 27, 28, 29, 31, **32**, 33,
  34, 38, **39**, 43,49, 60, **62**, 65, 67, 74, 75, 78,
  84, 91, **92**, 93, 94, 95, **96**, 97, **98**, 99, 100,
  102, 104, 106, 108, 109, 112, 116, **117**, 118,
  119, **120**, **121**, 122, 124, **126**, 127, **130**, **132**,
  134, 138, 139, 140, **141**, 143, 144, 146,
  148, 150, 151, 152
Chinese food 38
Chinese hemlock 24
Chinese invasion 9, 59, 93, 101, **106**, **131**,
  143, 146, 147, 151
Chinese language 30
Chinese medicine 34
Chinese occupation 94, 96, 143
Chinese officials 22, 32, 60, **96**, 97, 101,

102, 103, **104**
Chinese script **30**
Chiu Monastery **138**
Cho Oyu mountain 14, **15**, 144
Chökor Düchen 68, 147
Chomolungma Nature Preserve 22
Chomolungma, see Mt. Everest
Chonggye 134
Christians 51, 143
chromite 122, 146
chuba 40, 148
churn **38**, 45
circumnambulation 56, **57**, **111**, **114**
cities 27, 28, **29**, **38**, **136**
climate 17-20, 23, 145
clinics 34, 147
Clinton, Bill 109
cloth 45, 46, **62**, 149
cloth paintings 149
clothing 38, **39**, **40**, 42, 47, 146, 148
coal 146
colleges 132
Commander of 100,000 Warriors 72, 153
Commission of People's Deputies, see
   Assembly of Tibetan People's Deputies
communes **98**, **121**
communications 91, 126, 127, 146
Communist countries 99
Communist Party 93, 94, 116, 127
Communist principles 100
conch shells 65, 149
conifers 124
conservation 22, 25, 111, 145
constitution 111, 112, 143, 151
construction **85**, 97, 98, 126
convents 110
cooking 24, 41, **44**, 45, 59, 148
corn 146
Council of Ministers 115
County Rug Factory 136
crafts 62, 63
craftsmen 8, 31
creation myth 71
cremations 148
crops **19**, 23, 101, **120**, 146
cultural exchange 8, 147
Cultural Revolution 99, 134, 151
culture 11, 32, 51, 52, 53, 54, 91, 99, 110,
   113, 143, 147
curds 47
currency 144
customs 37, 38, 39, 40, 99, 148
cypress 145

dagger 40
daily life 8, 37, 38, 39, 40, 45, 51, 143
daimyo oak 24
Dalai Lama 7, 61, 62, 79, 80, 82, **83**, 84,
   85, 86, 87, 88, **89**, 90, 91, 93, 94, **95**, **96**,
   97, 98, 99, 100, 102, 103, 104, 105, **106**,
   107, **108**, 109, **111**, 112, **113**, 115, 124,
   127, 128, **130**, 131, 132, 135, 139, 140,

141, 143, 148, 150, 151, 152, 153
dance 65, 66, 68, 69, 94, 149
dance-drama 67, 147
Dancing Ghost Festival **66**
deer 19, 22, 35, 145
defense 115
deforestation 24, 145
deities 54, 55, 56, 61, 62, 63, **68**, 132, 143,
   147, 149
democracy 112, 141
democratic reforms 96, 97
demons 51, 65, 74
demonstrations 151, 152
Deng Xiaoping 101, 104
dental services **35**, 130
Denver, John **113**
Department of Education 147
Department of Information and
   International Relations 110, 113
Department of Religion and Culture 110
Department of Religious Affairs 115
Departments of Health 147
Derge 63, 139
desert 13, 17, **18**, 139
devotional practices 56, **57**, 58, 59
Dharamsala 61, **62**, **108**, 109, **110**, **111**, 127,
   146
dialects 29, 30, 31
diamond path 54
diseases 69, 117
doctors 34, 35, 100
dogs **45**, 47, **57**, 67, 98, 130
Dolma 17, 55, 143
domestic affairs 99, 102, 103, 115
donkeys 40, 121, 124, 146
doves 20, 145
dragons 130
Dram 137
dramas 68
Drapchi prison 102
Drepung Monastery, India 112, 149
Drepung Monastery, Tibet 68, 81, 82, 84,
   97, 112, 131, **132**, 150, 153
dress 38, 39, 40, 148
dri 47
drinking water 147
drokpa **13**, 44, **45**; see also nomads
Dromari Mountain 135
drums 8, 65, 149
Drung people 28
dung 146, 149
dungchen, see Himalayan long horns
Dunhuang 71
dzo 49

earrings 40
Earth Summit **113**
Eastern Turkestan 12
economy 115, 117, 118, 146
education 31, 32, 33, 147
eggs 22
Eight Auspicious Symbols 55, 56

Eight-Spoked Golden Wheel 56
Eightfold Path 53
electricity 41, **123**, 148
elements 66, 67, 143
eliminators 35
elm trees 23, 145
embalming 59
emperor 76, 78, 84, 85
endangered species **12**, 20, **22**, 25, 145
energy supplies 141
England 89, 109, 113
English 89, **126**, 127
Enlightened One, see Buddha
enlightenment 55, 68
environmental activist **113**
environmental protection zones 22
erosion 25
estates 90, 131
ethnic composition 143
European cities 112
evergreens 23, 24, 145
executions 101
executive branch 111, 143
exports 147

factories 119, 146
family 42, **43**, 148
famine 98
farm equipment 118, 120, 146
farm products 118, 119, 121
farmers 8, **98**, 121
farmhouse **41**
farming 27, 42, 101
farms 25, 97, 120, 121, 146
felt 48, 146, 148
fern 24
Festival to Banish Evil Spirits, see Year-
   End Festival
festivals **65**, 67, 68, **69**, 147
feudal system 89, 91
figwort 24
finger cymbals 65, 149
fir 24, 145
fish 20, **49**, 117
Five-Point Peace Plan 109
floods 19, 25
flour 37, 47, 148
flowers 9, 23, **43**, **137**
food 22, 23, 37, 38, 49, 149
foreign affairs 86, 93, 99, 102, 115
foreign investment 119, 141
forests 14, 19, 23, 24, 25, 98, 124, 145
Four Heavenly Kings 137
France 110, 112, 149
Franklin Delano Roosevelt Freedom
   Medal 152
Friendship Highway 137
fruit 38, 118, 147
fuel **24**, 48, 118, 146, 147, 149

Gampopa 76, 152
Ganden Monastery **79**, 81, 84, 112, **132**,

133, 149, 150
Ganden Palace 132
Ganges River 16, 138, 144
Gansu province 11, 71
gardens 53
Gate of Hell 138
gau 63, 149
gazelles 20, 140
Gedun Choekyi Nyima **104**
Gedun Drup 81, 82, 150, 152
Gedun Gyatso 81
Gelukpa sect 42, 79, 81, 82, 84, 106, 131, 132, 133, 140, 150, 153
Geneva 109
Genghis Khan 76, **77**, 149, 152, 153
geography 144
geothermal energy 123
Gesar 64, 147
Gesar, King 64
geysers **123**
ghosts 51
giant panda **12**, 22, 25
ginseng 24
goats 44, 121, 145, 146, 148
Godan 76, 149, 152
gods 47, 51, 55, 65
Golok people 28, **141**
gold 122, 130, 136, 146
golden pheasant 21
Golmud 125, 126, 140, 146
Gonggar International Airport 126, 146
gophers 20
government 27, 31, 84, 89, 93, 94, 115, 118, 143, 151
government officials 33, 90
government-in-exile 97, 109, 112, 113, 127, 143, 146, 147, 151, 152
grain 90, 119, 146
grasslands 20, 23, 144
grazing lands **121**
Great Britain, see Britain
Great Buddha Hall 135
Great Fifth 80, **83**, 84, 88, 152
Great Game 86, **87**
Great Prayer Festival, see Mönlam
griffon vultures 20
grunting ox, see yak
guerrilla fighters 94
Guge 75, 139, 153
Gurkha warriors 86, 150
Guru Rinpoche 74, 153
Gushri Khan 82, 83, 84, 150
gyaling, see trumpets
Gyantse 53, **69**, 89, 116, 126, **136**

habitat loss **25**
hair **39**, 40, 148
handicrafts 146, 149
Hanuman langur 21
hats 40, 61
hazardous waste 117

health 33, 34, 35, 110, 147
heart disease 33
hemlock 145
hemoglobin 33
Hengduan, see Khawakarpo mountain range
herbs 24, 35, 47, 145, 147, 148
hides 47, 49, 117, 146, 148
High Altar **81**
Himachal Pradesh 109
Himalayan long horns 65, 149
Himalayan marmot 20
Himalayan mouse hares 20
Himalayan raccoon, see red panda
Himalayas 7, 13, 14, 15, 19, 20, 24, 29, 96, 125, 138, 144, 146
Hindus 10, 138, 139, 143, 144
historical Tibet 11, 17, 24, 27, 28, 29, 120, 124, 126, 142, 145
holidays 67, 68, 69, 147
holy mountains **10**, 68
holy sites **17**, 56, **57**, 148
Hong Kong 97, 119
horses 121, 146
horns **60**, 65
hospitals 34, 93, 100, 147
hot-water springs 123
hotels **101**, 127, 131
household goods 118, 146
houses **41**, 42, **43**, 148, 149
Huangho River 25
Hui people 28, 51
human rights 99, 113, 141
Human Rights Caucus 108, 151
Human Rights Watch/Asia 113
humors 34
Hundred Thousand Songs 64
Hungary 110
hydroelectric plants 89, 123

ibex 20, **21**, 145
ICBM base 116, 146
illnesses 35, 51, 147
immigrant visas 152
immigration 119, 141
Imperial Preceptor 77, 153
imports 147
Incense Festival 68, 147
independence 88, 102, 108, 150
India 8, 12, 14, 16, 28, 29, 30, 52, 54, 61, **62**, 72, 73, 74, 75, 86, 87, 91, **95**, 96, 97, 99, **107**, **108**, 109, 110, 112, 116, 127, 132, 143, 144, 146, 147, 149, 151, 152, 153
Indian 15, 54, 109, 144, 150, 152
Indian subcontinent 12, 16, 112, 149
Indus River **16**, 25, 138, 145
industry 27, 34, 122, 118, 119, 139, 146
infant mortality 147
influenza 33, 147
ink 140
insects 20

intercontinental ballistic missile base 116, 146
International Campaign for Tibet 113
International Commission of Jurists 99, 151
international organizations 33, 141
international relations **32**, 99, 110
intonation 30
iron ore 122, 146
ironwork 146
irrigation 121

jade 122, 146
Jain 139
Jammu 86, 150
Jampa, see Maitreya
Jampalyang 54
Japan 54, 97, 109
jewelry 39, 40, 42, 130, 148
Jinsha Jiang River, see Yangtze River
Jokhang Temple 68, **73**, **74**, 96, 107, **114**, **128**, 129, **130**
Jowo Sakyamuni 129
judges 112
judicial branch 111, 143
juniper trees 24, 58, 145
Justice Commission 143

Kagyupa sect 76, 77, 82, 150, 152, 153
Kailas Range 15, 16, 145
Kalimpong. 126
kangling 65
Kangxi 85
Kangyur 64, 147
Karakoram Range 15, 144
karma 53
Karma Kagyud order 133
Karma sub-sect 82
Karmapa order 76, 82, 133, 152
Karnataka state 112
Kashag, see Council of Ministers
Kashmir 139
Kathmandu 109, 112, 125, 126
Kham province 11, 24, 27, 83, 88, 91, 93, 120, 124, 139
Khampa people 28, **39**, 40, 94, **95**, 139, 151
khata 58
Khawakarpo mountain range 15
kiang 20, **21**, 22
Korea 54
Kublai Khan 76, 77, 82, 133, 150, 153
Kumbum Monastery **59**, 106, 136, 140
Kunlun Mountains 15, 144
Kyichu, see Lhasa River
Kyichu Valley 133

Labor Day 147
Lake Kokonor 17, 79, 116, 140, 145, 146
Lake Manasarovar **17**, **138**, 145
lakes 13, 15, 16, 17, 20, 47, 132, **133**, 138,

140, 144, 145
lamas 52, 59, **61**, 62, 76, 77, 78, **79**, 82, 86, 91, 105, 106, 137, 148
lamb meat 37, 149
lamps 41, 47
Lancang Jiang, see Mekong River
Land of Snows 7, **9**, 19
landlords 59, 148
landslides 25, **125**
Langdarma 75, 153
language 29, 30, 31, 32, 94, 143, 151
langurs 19, **21**
Lanzhou 126
laws 78, 112, 148
lead 146
leaf-eating monkey, see Hanuman langur
leather 119
legislative branch 111, 112, 143
leopard 35
lesser panda, see red panda
lethal injection 100
Lhabab Düchen 69
Lhabzang Khan 85, 150
Lhamo Lhatso Lake 61, 105
Lhasa 8, 16, 17, 18, 26, 27, 28, 30, 33, 34, **35**, **40**, 51, **53**, 60, **63**, 67, 68, 71, **73**, 75, 76, 79, **80**, 84, **85**, 87, 89, 91, 94, 95, 96, 100, **101**, 102, 104, 106, 108, 112, **114**, 116, 119, 123, 124, 125, 126, 127, **128**, 129, 130, **131**, **132**, **133**, 135, 136, 138, 140, 143, 144, 146, 147, 150, 151, 153
Lhasa uprising **95**
Lhasa Apsos 98
Lhasa River 16, 23, 120
Lhatse 137, 138
Lhoba people 28
Lhoka district 122
Lhotse I 14, 144
Lhotse II 14, 144
libraries 71, 110, 130, 149
Library of Tibetan Works and Archives 110, 148
lichens 23, 24, 145
life expectancy 33, 147
Lingkhor 129
Lion Throne **89**
Litang Monastery 94, 151
literacy 31, 32, 147
literature 64, 65, 78, 110, 147, 148
lithium 122, 146
livestock 121, 146, 148
Lodi Gyari 104
London 109, 113
looms 45, **46**, 148
Lop Nor region 117, 151
Lords of the Four Directions 129
Losar 67, 147
Lotus Flower 55, 56
lynxes 19, 145

machinery 119, 146
magazines 127
magic 42
magnolia 24
Mahayana sect 54
Maitreya 54, 68, 132, 135
Makalu I 14, 144
Malaysia 119
Manchuria 84
Manchus 84-88, 150
mandala **56**, 147
Mandarin **30**, 31, 143
Mani stones **58**
Manjushri, see Jampalyang
mantra 56, 58
manufacturing 118, 146
manuscripts 97, 130
Mao Zedong 93, 99, 100, 151
Mapham Tso, see Lake Manasarovar
maple trees 23, 145
markets **38**, **114**, 130
Marpa 76, 153
marriage 42, 148
martens 19
martial law 103
masks 149
Master of Metaphysics 108
mastiffs **45**
meat 37, 38, 146, 148, 149
meat dumplings 37
medical centers 112
Medical College **96**, 151
medicinal herbs 24, 47, 117, 145, 147, 148
medicine 31, 33, 34, 35, 64, 147
meditation 54, 62, 84
Mekong River 16, 139, 145
Menri Monastery 52
merchant **63**
metalwork 63
metaphysics 31, 107
Mexico 113
mica 122, 146, 147
Milarepa 64, 76, 153
Milarepa's Cave 137
military 27, 94, 102, 116, 125, 126
militia duty 116
milk 47, 146
millet 146
mineral salts 17
minerals 118, 141, 146
Ming Dynasty 78, 84, 150
minibuses 125, 146
mining 118, 122, 126, 146
minstrels 66
modernization **89**, 91, 102, 118
Moinba people 28
momo 37
monasteries 8, 31, 33, 42, 52, **59**, **60**, 61, 65, 67, 68, 74, 75, 76, **78**, **81**, **90**, 91, **96**, 97, 102, 104, 105, 106, 110, 112, 115, 129, 131, **132**, **134**, 135, 136, 137, 139, 140,

143, 147, 148, 149, 151, 153
money 59, 88, 118, 144, 148, 149
Mongol overlords 76, 79
Mongolia 8, 17, 87, 144
Mongols 28, 76, **77**, 78, 82, 84, 85, 137, 140, 150, 152
monk-soldiers 59, 91
monkeys 19, 67, 71, 133, 145
monks 8, 40, 42, 58, **59**, **60**, 61, **64**, 65, 66, 67, **68**, 69, 71, 74, 75, 76, 77, 79, 84, 86, 90, 91, 94, 97, 100, 102, 104, 105, 106, 107, 112, **114**, 115, 131, 132, 133, **135**, 137, 139, 140, 147- 153
Mönlam 67, 68, 147, 153
monsoons **18**, **134**, 145
Moscow 109
mosses 23, 145
motor vehicles 119, 124
Mount Gongbori 133
mountain passes 8, **29**, 97, 138
mountains 4, **6**, 7, 11, 12, 13, **14**, **15**, **16**, **18**, 19, **21**, **25**, 51, 56, 139, 144, 146
mountainsides 20, 41, **78**, 125, 131, 145
moxibustion 35
Mt. Everest **4**, 14, 144
Mt. Kailas **10**, 17, **138**, 139, 144
mudslides 19, 146
mugwort 35
mules 121, 146
multiphonic singing 66
municipalities 115
murals 83, **85**, 129, 134, 136, 137, 139
museum 131
music 65, 149
musical instruments **8**, **60**, **65**, 149
musk deer 19, 22, 35, 145
Muslims **40**, 51, 143
Mustagh, see Karakoram Range
mustard **19**
Myanmar 12, 144

Nagchu prefecture 116
naked carp 20
Nam Tso (lake) 17, 132, 145
Nam Tso Bird Sanctuary 22
Namri Songtsen 72, 152, 153
Nan Shan mountains 15, 17
National Assembly 115
national epic, see Gesar
Nationalist Chinese government 93
nature spirit worship, see animism
Naxi people 28
Nechung Monastery (India) **108**
Nechung Monastery (Tibet) **103**, 132
Nechung Oracle 61, 132
Nepal 8, **12**, 14, **15**, 28, 29, 52, 72, 86, 96, 109, 110, 112, 116, **125**, 126, 134, 136, 137, 144, 147, 149, 150, 152
Nepal-Tibet Highway 125, 146
New Delhi 109, 127
New Year festival **68**, 94, 147

New York 104, 109, 152
newspaper 127, 146
Ngari 116, **117**, **138**
Ngawang Lobsang Gyatso, see Great
    Fifth
nirvana 53, **55**, 139
Nobel Peace Prize 103, 151, 153
Noble Eightfold Path 56
nobles 79, 84, 90
nomads 8, 12, **13**, **14**, **26**, 27, **28**, **32**, 33,
    38, 42, **44**, **45**, **46**, 47, 48, 49, 71, 115, **121**,
    122, **130**, 139, 140, 148, 149, 152
noodle broth 38, 149
Norbulingka Palace 68, 95, 96, **130**, 131
Northern Plain 13
northern plateau 44, 136
Nu people 28
nuclear facilities 34, 116, 146, 147
nuclear tests 117, 151
Nujiang, see Salween River
nuns 8, 59, **60**, 100, 102, 104, 110, 152, 153
nurses 34
Nyalam 137
Nyatri Tsenpo 72, 134, 153
Nyingchi prefecture 116
Nyingmapa order 76, 153

oak trees 23, 145
oboes 65, 149
Ocean of Wisdom, see Dalai Lama
ogress 133
oleanders 23
Opium War 86
oracle 61, 132
orchards 131
Outer Plateau 14, 23, 144
overpopulation 42
oxen 20
oxygen 33, **34**, 37

Padmasambhava 64, 73, 74, 76, 135, 153
palaces 151
Palkhor Chöde monastery 136
Panchen Lama 61, 62, 91, 99, 100, 102,
    103, **104**, 135, 150, 151, 152
pandas **12**, 19, 22, **25**, 145
pansies 23
parliamentary democracy 109
pastoral nomads, see drokpa
pastureland 44, 45, 47, 121, 122, 131, 148
patron-priest relationship 76, 150
peace treaty 74
pearls 134
peas 37, 146, 149
peasants **24**, **90**, 91
People's Congress 116
People's Courts 116
People's Daily 127
People's Liberation Army **92**, 93, 116
People's Republic of China 11, 28, 93,
    115, 116, 143

performing arts 65, 66, 110
Phagpa 77, 153
philosophy 31, 64, 107
Phuntsok Nyidron 104, 152, 153
pikas 20
pilgrimages **10**, **130**, 138, 139
pilgrims **29**, 56, **57**, **58**, 67, 68, 69, **74**, 94,
    111, **114**, **128**, 129, 132, 138, 140
pine trees 23, 124, 138, 145
pipits 20
PLA, see People's Liberation Army
Place of the Gods, see Lhasa
plains 13, **15**, 144
plants 23, 24, 25
plateau **5**, 11, **12**, **13**, **14**, 20, 23, 28, **44**,
    47, 49, 117, 123, 125, 134, 144
plumbing 42, 148
plutonium 146
pneumonia 33, 147
poet 64, 76, 137, 153
police 91, 104, 130
political boundaries 11, 124
political freedom 94, 151
political power 77
political prisoners 103
pollution 116
ponies 121, 124, 146
poplar trees 145
population 27, **28**, 100, 144
porcelain 147
post offices 127
Potala Palace **26**, **80**, 84, **85**, **96**, 105, **128**,
    130, 131, 153
potatoes 120, 146
pottery 63, 149
power plants 94
prayer flags 56, **57**
prayer pole 137
prayer scrolls 63
prayer wheels 56, **57**, 130, 148
prayers 56, 57, 58, **103**, **128**, 148
precious metals 63
precipitation 18, 145
prefectures 116, 143
president 112
priest-doctors 42, 51
prime ministers 108, 115, 143
printing 65, 139, 140
prison 97, 151, 152
prostrations 56, **57**, **114**
protectorate 85
protests 102
provinces 115
public transportation 125, 146
pulses 35
Purang 75, 138

Qiang people 28
Qing Dynasty 84, 87, 150
Qinghai Lake, see Lake Kokonor
Qinghai province, see Amdo Province

Qinghai-Tibet Highway 125, 146

radio 127, 146
Radio Lhasa 127
radioactive nuclear wastes 117
radium 146
railroads 126, 146
rain 18, **19**, 71
rainy season 17, **18**
Ralpachen 74, 75, 153
Ramoche temples 73
rapeseed 146
Reagan, Ronald 109
recreation 149
Red Guards 99
Red Hats 76, 149
Red Hill 84, **128**, 130
red pandas 19, **25**, 145
Reebok Human Rights Award 104, 152,
    153
refugees 33, 52, 94, 97, 110, 112, 113,
    147, 149, 152
regional municipality 116, 143
Regional People's Congress 116
reincarnation 40, 53, 61, 62, 81, 103, 105,
    106, 133, 148, 152
religion 31, 51, 52, 53, 54, 55, 56, 77, 93,
    96, 97, 102, 107, 122, 139, 143
religious dramas 65, 66
religious education 31, 59, 75, 106, 147
religious festivals 102, 140, 151
religious freedom 94, 102, 141, 151
religious objects 40, 63, 97, 149
religious sects 9, 77
religious texts 81, 153
Republican Revolution 87
resources 109, 122, 124, 141, 145
restaurants 38, 119, **126**
retail shops 119
revenue 115
rhesus macaques 19
rhododendrons **23**, 24, 145
rice 38, 47, 98, 118, 120, 146, 147, 148
rickshaws 125, 146
Rinpoche 61
river valleys 14, 23, 27, 124, 144
rivers **5**, **12**, **14**, 15, **16**, 17, 19, 20, 24, 25,
    56, 69, 123, 138, 144, 145
roads 25, 93, 94, 118, 122, 124, **125**, 135,
    138, 146
robes 61
robins 20, 145
rodents 20
Rombok Monastery **4**
Roof of the World 11, 144
ropes 146
rosary beads 58, 106, 148
royal decrees 71
ruddy shelducks 20
rugs 45, **63**, 149
Russia 86, 87, 99, 109

Rutok 75

sacred music 149
saddles 48, 149
Sahara Desert 124
Sakadawa 68
Sakya lama 137
Sakya Monastery 76, 136, 149
Sakya Pandita 76, 77, 149, 150
Sakya Valley **78**, **90**, **137**
Sakyamuni 54, 68
Sakyapa sect 76, 77, 137, 149, 150, 152
salt 37, **38**, 47, 122, 14-148
Salween River 16, 145
Sambhota 134
Samye Monastery **50**, 74, 83, **134**, 135, 153
Sangye Gyatso **83**, 84
Sanskrit 30, 64, 73, 74, 153
Santarakshita 73, 74, 135, 153
scholar-saints 135
scholars 8, 73, 76, 79, 84, 107, 149, 152, 153
school **31**, 32, 89, 93, 110, 112, 147
scribes 59
script 30, 73, **74**, 153
scriptures 54, 107, 140, 149, 152
scroll trumpets **65**
sculptures 47, 63
secular music 66
seminary 151
Sera Monastery **55**, 81, 82, 84, 96, 106, 112, **132**, 149, 150
serfs 90
seven-leafed grass 24
seventeen-point plan 151
Shalu Monastery **114**
Shamanism 51
shamans 42, 51
Shambhala **6**, **7**, **9**
Shangri-La, see Shambhala
Shannan prefecture 116
sheep **13**, 44, **46**, 63, 67, 117, 121, 130, 136, 140, 146, 148
sheepskin 40, 46, 148
shepherds 14
Shigatse 23, **29**, **41**, 52, 76, **78**, 81, 82, **98**, 116, 125, **135**, 136, 144
Shiquanhe 139
shoes 39, 63, 149
shopping 31, **35**, **113**
Shötun, see Yogurt Festival
shrines 56, 59, 67
Sichuan food 38
Sichuan province 11, 12, 124, 126, 139, 144
Siddhartha Gautama 52
signs **30**
Sikkim 8, 72, **107**, 112, 149
silk 147
silt 25

silver **39**, 122, 130, 146
Simla Conference 88, 150
Sinkiang Uighur 12
sky burial 58
slingshots 47, 48, **49**, 146
snow finches 20, 145
snow grouse 20, 145
snow leopards 19, **22**, 145
snow lion 20
snow pig, see Himalayan marmot
snowline 19, 144
social welfare 149
socializing **44**, 148
soil 17, 25, 34
solar energy 123, 124
soldiers 104
Sonam Gyatso 82, 150, 153
songbirds 98
Songtsen Gampo 30, 72, 73, 78, 80, 84, 129, 134, 152, 153
souvenirs 101
spirit world 51
spirits 52, 58, 61, 68, 69, 122, 143
spiritual center 129, 140
spiritual enlightenment 53, 54
spiritual exercises 54, 56, 147
spiritual leader 105, 107, 115, 153
spiritual poisons 34, 35
spruce trees 24, 145
squirrels 19, 145
Sri Lanka 54
stamps 88
starvation 98, 101
statues 41, 45, **55**, 58, 63, 129, 130, 132, 134-137
steppes 140
sterilization 100
storytellers 64
stove **41**
Strasbourg Proposal 151
streams 42, 51
students **101**
stupas 62, 75, 106, 131, 136, 140
subtropical regions 24
sugar 118, 147
sugar beets 146
Sui Dynasty 72
sunbirds 20
Supreme Court 112
Supreme Justice Commission 109
Sutlej River 16, 138
swans 20, 145
Switzerland 109, 112, 149
symbols 54, 55, 56, 63, 147

Taiping Rebellion 86
Taiwan 119
Tamdrok Yumtso 145
T'ang dynasty 71
Tanggula Mountains 140
tannery 119, 146

tantras 54
tantrism 54, 74
TAR, see Tibet Autonomous Region
Tara, see Dolma
Tashilhunpo Monastery 81, **135**, 150, 152
taxes 78, 84, 90, 91
tea 24, **26**, **38**, 47, 101, 145, 147, 148, 149
technical schools 147
technicians 27, 118
telecommunications 126
telegraph 88, 126, 150
telephone service 126, 127
television 127, 146
temperatures 18
temples **8**, **52**, 62, 63, 67, 68, 75, 84, 129, 131, 134, **135**, 140
Tengyur 64, 147
tents **44**, 45, 46, 47, 48, 149
Tenzin Gyatso 105, 153
Tethys Sea 13, 17
textiles 63, 118, 119, 146, 147
thangkas **62**, 68, **69**, 129, 149
theater 131
theocracy 115
Theravada sect 54
Thöling 139
Thonmi Sambhota 30, 73, 153
thukpa **38**, 149
Thupten Gyatso 88, 89, 153
Tibet Autonomous Region 11, 12, 15, 17, 27, 32, 99, **101**, 116, 120, 121, 122, 124, 125, 126, 139, 141, 143, 147, 151
Tibet Daily 127, 146
Tibet Information Network 113
Tibet TV 127
Tibet University 33, 147
Tibetan Bulletin 113, 127
Tibetan Children's Village 111
Tibetan Institute of Performing Arts 110
Tibetan Library 110
Tibetan Medical and Astro. Institute 110, 148
Tibetan Medical Center 34, 147
Tibetan Plateau 13, 14, 15, 20, 46, **48**, 63, 116, 121, 122, 127
Tibetan Review 113, 127
Tibetan rose finches 20
Tibetan Youth Conference 151
Tibeto-Burman people 28
Tibeto-Burman language group 29, 143
tigers 19, 35, 67, 145
timber 118, 124, 141, 145
tin 146
Tingri **15**, **24**
Tokyo 109
tombs 131, 134
tomden 58, 59
topography 12, 14
torture 101

tourism 60, **101**, 104, 130, 143, 149, 151
tractors **98**, **120**, 121, 125
trade 47, 86, 87, 146, 147, 151
trade agreements 108, 150
traditional medicine 20
trance 51
Trandruk Temple 134
transportation **26**, **31**, 91, **120**, 124, **125**, 146
treasures 129, 130, 134
treaties 99
trees **23**, 24, 25, 145
tribesmen 130
Trisong Detsen 73, 74, 135, 149, 152
trucks **98**
trumpets 149
tsampa 37, 149
Tsang kings 82, 150
Tsang princes 150
Tsang province 82, 135, 136, 150
Tsangpo River Valley **19**
Tsaparang 139
Tsetang **50**, **70**, 71, 72, 133, 134, 135
tsi-tog 23
Tsong Khapa 68, 69, 79, 81, 106, 133, 140, 153
Tsurphu Monastery 82, 133
tuberculosis 33, 147
Turkic people 12, 75
turquoise **39**, 40, 63, 148
Two Golden Fishes 56

Ü-Tsang 11, 120, 122
U.S. Congress 108, 113, 151, 152
U.S. State Department 109
United Nations 94, 99, 104, 151, 152
United States 113, 119, 149, 152
universities 59, 74, 148, 151, 153
uranium 122, 146
usnea lichen 24

Vajrapani, see Chakna Dorje
Valley of the Kings 134
valleys 13, 19, 25, 133, **134**, 144
vegetable dyes 63
vegetables 37, 38, 149
violins 66
vocal techniques 65, 66
Voice of America 127, 152
vultures **58**, **59**, 145, 148

warlords 84
Washington, D.C. 113
water **14**, 34, 37, 41
water pollution 34
waterfalls 138
wealth **39**, 40
weapons 65, 88
weaving **46**, 148
Wencheng 72, 153
wheat **98**, 120
wheateaters 20
Wheel of Time 66
white-lipped deer 22
wild asses, see kiangs
wild horses 20
wild yaks 98, 145
wildlife **12**, 19, 20, **21**, **22**, 23, 25, 35, 40, **45**, 46, 47, 49, **57**, 67, 71, 98, 121, 122, 124, 130, 133, **135**, 140, 145, 146
willow trees 24, 145
winter wheat 146
women **26**, **38**, 39, 46, 100, 148
wood **24**, 98
wood carvings 63, 149
wool 40, **46**, 47, 48, 63, 117, 136, 147, 148
Working Committee 115
writing 30, 134

Xining 105, 126, 140
Xinjiang Autonomous Region 12, 139, 144
Xizang, see Tibet Autonomous Region

yak butter 37, **38**, 45, 47, 71, 130, 148
yak curds 38, 149
yak dung 41, 45, 48
yak hair **39**, 44, 46, **49**
yak herder 126
yak hides **39**, 48, **49**, 63
yak meat 37, 47, 48, 130, 148, 149
yak-butter candles 41, 129
yak-butter lamps 45, 69, 81, 123, 149
yak-butter sculptures **61**, 68, **87**
yak-butter tea 37, **38**, 47, 149
yaks 22, **26**, **28**, 44, 45, **46**, 47, 48, 49, 98, 121, 124, 136, 145, 146, 148, 149
Yambulakang **70**
Yamdrok Tso (lake) **12**, 17, 123, **133**, 135
Yangtze River 16, 25, 139, 145
Yarlung kings **70**, 72, 73, 74, 75, 78, 133
Yarlung Tsangpo River 7, 15, **16**, 25, 27, 123, 134, 135, 138, 144
Yarlung Valley **71**, 72, 120, 124, 133
Year-End Festival 69
Yellow Hats 81, 153
Yellow River, see Huangho River
Yeshe Ö 75, 153
yogurt 37, 47, 48, 148, 149
Yogurt Festival 68
yoncho, see patron-priest relationship
Younghusband, Colonel Francis 87
yuan 118, 144
Yuan Dynasty 77, 150
Yuan emperors 77
Yuan Shikai 88
Yumbu Lakang castle **70**, 133
Yungdrung Ling monastery 52
Yunnan province 11, 12, 124, 144

Zen Buddhism 74
Zhangmu 137
zinc 146

About the Author

Ann Heinrichs grew up in Arkansas and lives in Chicago. She is the author of twelve books on American and Asian regions and cultures, as well as numerous newspaper, magazine, and encyclopedia articles. In the advertising and marketing fields, her subjects have ranged from plumbing hardware to Oriental rugs. In private life, Ms. Heinrichs is a classical pianist, a desert traveler, and a student of t'ai chi standard and sword forms.